The Act of fact

Kaushalam Foundation NGO®

Non Government Organisation

ಆಶಿಪ್ಟೋ ಬಲಿಪ್ಟೋ ದೃಢಿಷ್ಠಃ

Ambition Strength Determination

Dr. Chandra Mouli M S

: Dedicated to :

My Parents

Ve||Br||Shree||Suryanarayana M A

Sangita Vidushi||Manjula H S

Contents

Entry

There is a supreme wish behind this ultimate creation
There is a supreme gut behind his ultimate celebration
Our great father sacrificed everything for our protection
He is free to act because of the truth in his function |1|

Truth is the force behind the greatest manifestation
But the reasons are the key to its functional organization
If a person foregoes the fruits of all his deeds
He can escape from those organisational seeds |2|

Vedic vibration can be conceived in two major ways
Because it has its own unique existence with brilliant rays
Vedic hymns always move as a principle in physiological evolution
They have the ability to even cause a psychological revolution |3|

The inner meanings of mantras will flow freely in the poetry
Constructively, it actuates the essences of truth with symmetry
Because of this, local structures should not neglect it outwardly
Understand, this is the path to the unknown from the known, inwardly |4|

The actuality of the mantra is maintained in exclusive form
They obey the norm when they enter the local realm
However, the functionality of them depends on physical reality
But they move differently when they enter an emotional formality |5|

The principle of speech is unique to the sentence of local existence
Humans hone their intrinsic voices in order to persist in Ruta's surveillance
Their poetic genesis is based on the fundamental flow of their inner voice
The emotion morphosis depends on the meaning of the Vedic choice |6|

The stones communicate in a Pashyanti kind of cosmic order
The trees and plants communicate in a Madhyama manner
Human minds will be able to communicate in a Vaikhari direction
But the Vedic mantras communicate according to Ruta's instruction |7|

Proper delicacy will be born of good steward within us
Moving in humility will bring politeness with good focus
Because of these qualities, man will progress in his own nature
But if one moves in contrast to his nature, he will rot in the future |8|

The creation of pure consciousness is amazingly very vast
Vim first appeared in the Vishwam before the long known past

Good, bad, and ugly are all just inventions of our imaginary kind
Aversion is never encouraged, so please update your mind |9|

The fundamentals of creativity manifest with the proper sound
But remember, it will never support the local polluted mind
The air will gain momentum in sound with proper pronunciation
Internal tools will be supported by grammatical error renunciation |10|

The white in the world always emanates colour of every kind
Speech is able to absorb every moment of the inner mind
There is no such thing as a thought that cannot observe sound
As Brahma moves in name, he moves in the formation bound |11|

Communication in humans has particular busyness norms
Its direct and indirect modes will be based on emotional forms
These modes' symptoms are the order of fundamental creativity
The consonants of this busyness are concerned with vowel flexibility |12|

The thought prefix is imbibed in Para communication
Internal thoughts will sprout in Pashyanti's unification
The manifestation of sentences is in the form of Madhyama mode
Inspiration for the tongue lies in the Vaikhari communication node |13|

The movement of creativity is like a cool water flow
It will become personal in the realm of self-religious glow
It will move in pure form through the poster of moodiness
To gain this, one has to overcome their selfish crudeness |14|

For creativity, the Om-kara is the most primitive form
It was allotted to three then for the local usage norm
So, the chanting of Om is the fundamental need for non-local reverberation
The earth, space, and sun foundations are there for local creative
formation|15|

Creativity is there in the land to grow beyond this universe
Sensitivity will appear to help us understand the internal multiverse
Creativity is nothing more than the realisation of inner potential norms
This is an exit from local to non-local with supreme maturity corns' |16|

This world has been under measurement since the age of unknown
Because of this, the life born here is always bonded to the cruel dun
The slavery born of the bond will grind this life to its maximum extent
So one has to overcome this measurement with creative up-liftment |17|

The four Vedic systems originated for the sake of creativity
Then eight limbs were born for the sake of giving maturity
The forms of vowels were designed for their local sensibilities
The Swa-Dharma arranged consonants for their local realities |18|

The initial form of creativity is just in non-local potentiality
It will become sensible to the locality by its name formality
Bringing it to the realm of attributes is the first step towards its manifestation
It will be actualized then, with the help of the principles of Vedic synthesisation |19|

Creativity has many vertical dimensions in this universe
There are seven layers, from the lowest to the highest levels
However, just the rationality of the intellect can't compile this
However, anyone can achieve this by using a springboard of bliss |20|

If one becomes a slave to this world, it will certainly crush him
If anyone tries to rule this world, it will certainly push him
So, transcending this world is the only true solution
So be prepared to gain certainty with proper resolution |21|

There is a Gnyanam for Ucchranam in Shiksham for creativity
There is a Nirvachanam for Shabdam in Niruktam for relativity
Vyakaranam is there in the domain of Shabdam for their movements
Chandus is there for the domain of the limbs of creative statements |22|

Jyotisham and Kalpam are related to the action of substances
So they will capture the forms of creativity with resonances
Jyotisham will explain the actuality of the stuff of creativity
Vani is the actual connection that ensures creative functionality |23|

Dharma with Guhya, Shrouta, and Shilpa narrates the creative formulas
Shilpa explains only the sacrificial platforms for the fundamental creators
If the Guhya explains Samskara and the Dharma directs the practices
The Shrouta demonstrate the speech and behaviour of the sacrificers |24|

The Puranas narrate the basic principles of creativity
The Dharma Shastra explains the systems of conductivity
The pulchritude of basic creativity is narrated in the form of a story
Creativity moves perfectly only in the realm of pure system glory |25|

The vision of the Vedic Rishi is a sort of Pushpak Vimanam
At the consonant fair, it is a grant by the vowel's curriculum

The Apourusheyam is the inspiration born of great beings
This is the Pourusheyam for the poet with the subtle humming's |26|

Creativity lies in explicit, subtle, and dormant consesalities
This depended on Bhu, Bhuvaha, and Suvaha's peculiarities
The essence of creativity flows in the vibrancy of local activity
Because of many linkages, the leakiness occurs in its subjectivity |27|

The essence of creativity is never diluted due to the flow of time
Instead, it flows more ferociously with the help of Sattvic mime
Remember, the cuckoo's singing never fades away in time limitation
Thus, the vowel of creativity moves along with the bud of sublimation |28|

The practise and penance are gift for a life to become that
It aids in capturing connections with the feel of the gut
Keep in mind that it is not a matter of repeated damnations
Yes, it is possible if one grasps the charm with preparations |29|

The probabilities of creativity are in infinite names and forms
Locals have to find the possibilities of it by giving up selfish norms
For the sake of research, one has to understand self-religiousness
It will become possible only then by moving in righteousness |30|

The explicit needs to be understood in the realm of truth
The implicit folds must be undertaken with a sense of oath
The speech of the creator will become pure by local segregation
His feelings will be complete because of the non-local aggregation |31|

For the sake of creativity, one should brush up on their grammar
One should scrub the surface of his emotions with a Satt scrubber
Then, his consciousness will actualise the probability of creation
Individualisation occurs then, but only with complete dedication |32|

The dimension of Sankhya moves through three para-normalities
It includes differentiality, integrality, and integrated visualities
Accomplishments with a reason and function are necessities for creation
Otherwise, the efficacy of creativity certainly takes the wrong direction |33|

In the presentation of the efficacy of macros, there is mathematics
There is a platform for the efficacy of micro-behavioural statistics
One can explain the micro and macro forms with the support of Pourusheyam
But to narrate the subtle probabilities, he needs true kind of
Apourusheyam|34|

Every person has distinct perceptions of knowledge and deeds
In addition, everyone has ego, mood, and mind tools
So, he can use a tool of speech to express his objective
If he prefers, he can increase his chances of being creative |35|

External science will be born of the intellect in a linear fashion
But inner science will be born of intelligence in circular motion
Because of the linear mode, it just moves in the local physical dimension
But the circular one flows from dormant to subtle with potential
animation|36|

The forms of creativity move through space prudently
Like the names of that this moves in time, efficiently
However, the names are more prominent in creative forms
Still, potential extends its hands beyond both of its norms |37|

With the seven Chandus, the Gayatri is there for creativity
This will reach the earth with the rays of Aditya for actuality
These deluges are granted for the sake of non-local objectivity
In Vyahurti, with the Agni, one can actualise its fundamentality |38|

Due to Sama Ganam, the potential will become embossed
From the inner flow of Atharva Mantram, it will become composed
Because of the Vani of the Ruk, it moves in the desired direction
Only when one constructs it with the help of the Yajur Yagnic oblation |39|

For the sake of creativity, there should be an aptitude on hand
There should be proper observation as the next supportive strand
Because of the heat born of suffering, aptitude will be born implicitly
Due to the refinement born of yoga, creativity shines explicitly |40|

Through its implicit essence, pure consciousness does the creation
Just like the spider will weave its web from its inner secretion
Therefore, there is a need for true inner essence for local creation
So, emotions should flow freely within, without the feeling of separation |41|

The analysis born of intellect in creativity is due to differentiation
However, the synthesis in creativity is an action of divine proportion
So, if the analysis is not included by the person in his creative action,
the synthesis will add juice with the help of Soma's secretion |42|

One should consider fundamental creativity to be their child
One should give everything to it, though, romping in the wild

Then, the analysis will start to fade away gradually from one's mind
And the essence of feeling begins to synthesise on poetic ground |43|

The secret of creativity is the movement of truth in eternal sensuality
Inside our thoughts, this is the function with the greatest capability
One can crack this secret with the help of their basic rationality
However, keep in mind that one must enjoy it while realising divinity |45|

In the pure science of creativity, there is a kind of curiosity
In the process of it, there is a pure form of witness authority
There is an advantage in the creative science of sincerity
There is a movement of purity in the deeds of its actuality |46|

The creative principal's knowledge is actually pure science
Its karmic haulm is, locally, a true technological quince
In terms of creativity, the science of intellect is not revelation
Instead, the science of its intelligence is a true gift of salvation |47|

The details of action are discussed in the Tattva shastra of basic creativity
This will tell you that one should leave the fruits to escape from the locality
Otherwise, the fruit will push life into the logical intellect again and again
But pure intelligence will not return life to this mortal domain once again |48|

The principle of creativity should be observed from Dhi's eye
The movement of it should be witnessed through Chit's sky
The internal eye is an essential part of the art of creativity
The pure local witness form is the protection of its religiosity |49|

No life forms have touched the limits of creativity till date
No formation was ever completed for every creative in state
Anyhow, one has to actualize it only through their own religiosity
However, one should think twice before touching its fundamentality |50|

For creativity, one has to understand its expanse primarily
Then they have to convert that into subjectivity, internally
The creator can use this for establishment purposes then
They can only actualize it then with the help of Kalpam's fun |51|

The Gnyana-Kandam of creativity is always subtle
The Karma-Kandam of it is vast because of its detail
However, the Upasana-Kandam is relatively glamorous
The efficaciousness of it is like a cow tail's glomerulus |52|

Knowledge of fundamental creativity starts with differentiality
Then it will move from integrality to the realm of singularity
Life residing in space and time is the reason for all this
Anyway, it will manifest through transition only in bliss |53|

The beginning of creativity starts with the realm of duality
It reaches its ultimatum only after passing through integrality
The results of it are always born from the source of singularity
Because its flow always resides in the potential of its non-locality |54|

Local desire is the main reason behind creativity
The pure mind is the platform for creative activity
The sacrificial witness of the creator is the actual foundation
Determination is the ingredient of his creative actualisation |55|

Along with ready ones, there are possible and determined personalities
If one is possible, then the ultimatum will be ready for their formalities
Only one's thoughts will suffice to determine one's external actualities
But the knowledge is required for possible executors to know internalities |56|

The resource of fundamental creativity is not all materialistic
So, it never depends on potential and energy to be futuristic
But the possible ones have to depend on the potency of nature
So they have to meditate on energy for their creative future |57|

All kinds of fundamental creativity are fully filled with purities
The efficacy of this is the play of inertia with particular functionalities
The absence of five fundamental materials is the reason for this purity
But it will move because of the efficacy of time and spatial locality |58|

The Sattva of creativity never interferes with our lives
The creativity in the Rajas comes with hate tune vibes
If it is in Tamas, it fills the soft spot in the local sensibility
As a result, one must use creativity in its purest causality |59|

This Sattva is essential for any kind of creative kama
This Kama follows the Rajasic and Tamasic Dharma
But the meaning follows the essence in a righteous way
So, to understand its basics is difficult in an explicit way |60|

Primarily, creativity will collapse from the unknown to the known, intrinsically
Individualization of it will be actualized in the domain of Swa-Dharma
secondarily

Actual formation is caused by touch, colour, smell, sound, and juices
The gross will then emerge from formation with its material process |61|

The cosmic order of creativity is the actual meaning of mind
The truth of this is the meaning of vocal 'functional wind'
These two aspects will manifest themselves in the work of creativity
The things born of Tapas are the expression of its fundamentality |62|

The penance is no different from the reality of radical creativity
The nonphysical form of formality is the instinct for its functionality
The truth and cosmic order will come together to support this sincerity
With fidelity, purity will descend into this domain, and then for sensitivity |63|

Many forms of reputation are present in the creative world
Both direct and indirect references will be realised in this mould
Though it is present, sometimes it acts as if it is really absent
Though it is absent, sometimes it moves as if it is fully present |64|

The opera without fascination is an example of creativity in Sattvic nature
However, the creativity with fondness comes with the Rajasic feature
But one should not always create anything with a Tamasic nature
Everyone should think before they act about this world's future |65|

For the sake of this world, creativity will shimmer from the jungles
This will move secretly from the bottom of the ocean for the locals
The opportunity of creativity oxidises the Apourusheyam of Nada
So, one has to observe these with the help of Pourusheyam of Veda |66|

Without the hull, it is impossible to protect the Phalam
Like that, without inertia, it is impossible to collect the Saaram
Oh man, please don't ignore these good, bad, ugly things in your lives
And develop your creative nature by considering these as virtual wives |67|

The results never arose just because the person executed the Karma of creativity
The fruits will never be realised because one has Gnyana in terms of fundamentality
Therefore, one has to move his mind to the witness part of the self with purity
Then one can actualise anything along the lines of Karma and Gnyana in clarity|68|

Life with its lord and his world are the traits of basic creativity
The bond and the liberation are the fruits of its fundamentality

With this individuality, the flow of creativity rages in this radicality
Coming is bondage, and going is the liberation from its actuality |69|

By retaining the intelligence of Vedic science, there is theistic creativity
By mining the intellect of external science, there is an atheist orgumentality
So, the intelligent always search for the potential in the realm of the self
But the intellect always seeks the proof of creativity on the outer shelf |70|

The Muni always tries to find a witness for creativity in self-religiousness
But the scientist tries to find evidence for his findings in outer worldliness
So, the devotee surrenders himself to the Mahat for the sake of revelation
But others reject everything other than ego for the sake of progression |71|

Intellect can be used to search the ground for the chain of causes
Intelligence is useful to see the art forms of radical creative clauses
The scientific form of creativity can coordinate life in a local sense
But the Mahat principle integrates the mind with nonlocal suspense |72|

In a local sense, one has to learn the art of creativity initially
Then one should understand the common science behind it logically
All these things are truly necessary to actualise our own creative forms
So, at the end of the journey, one can get hold of its poetic norms |73|

There should be an inquiry before taking up any act of creativity
With proper reasoning, one should touch the source of its nativity
The abandonment of scepticism may shed light on its gravity
Only then can one actualise his opus of creativity under affinity |74|

The Vedic scientists had already observed the fundamentals of creativity
They told us that one can catch its essence in pure perception activity
But mind it; the science in Vedic hymns is not at all beyond questioning
One can find facts with effort by aligning themselves with pure functioning|75|

Nucleus is the well-balanced debouche for creativity
This will provide everything for its embryo's activity
From the navel of Paraman, the vast is expressed as the cosmos
So, from it, the stuff for creativity will emerge with a full toss |76|

The creator will preserve this world with his pure sacrifice
So the world protects him by giving him a practical price
In give and take policy, this creative business is balanced well
But remember, this process is always held in a sacrificial shell |77|

Sama

One should practise Dharma and should speak the truth
One should offer good things to the teacher in good faith
One should not ignore the discourse with study at any cost
When one has this treasure, their fate will shine very fast |1|

One should not ignore the work of a true intelligent seeker
One should never neglect the father, mother, or teacher
One should treat the wise and guests as equivalent to god
Then the door of heaven opens for one who is not a fraud |2|

One should listen to the words of the person who knows Bruh-man
The Seeker should sit attentively in front of the wise as a true-man
Then one should grasp the knowledge of the wise with awareness
Every seeker should pay close attention to pure Gynani's fairness |3|

Penance

Observing the cosmic order as well as listening to the great truth
Conducting sacrifices along with oblation, controlling the mind & senses
Fixing Paraman as a goal in Upasana is the true meaning of one's Dharma
Observing Brahman as obvious in Vyahrutis will be his Tapasic Karma |1|

The truth is supreme, and the truth is always paramount
During the celebration of this, never promote the discount
Because of this observance, local life will never be degraded
If one pursues the truth in his walk of life, he will be upgraded |2|

There is compression from the lie, but there is expansion from the truth
Because he opened his eyes, the savant received amplification from its knuth
We should understand that by destining the truth, one can get an ultimatum
By adopting the ultimatum, the saints will get liberation from the self-
stratum|3|

Dharma

Reliance on the Tattvam is the true way to practice pure devotion
By rationalizing, one can gain true knowledge through promotion
Moving in the actual sense of "self-religion" is the way to liberation
True knowledge combined with pure devotion is the way to salvation |1|

Getting the meaning by the propulsion is called "self-religiousness"
Obtaining prosperity from self-religious requires the proper rituals
Misadventure will never be good for any kind of human being
Moving into humanity is actually the gist of religious seeing |2|

The art of creation

Before this entire creation, the darkness was in scope
It covered everything in free movement, with a loop
Therefore, Tamas is totally encapsulated by real subtlety
But everything will be published under the Tapas' fidelity |1|

Before this entire creation, lust was in every place
In reality, this phenomenon was the first in the race
The revolutionary scientists inquired about this again and again
And realised the Tattva of publication from the unpublished domain |2|

For the sake of creation, one should conduct Agni-Hotram in their house
One should offer oblation for the sake of expiation with their spouse
Good class is defined as achieving goals through proper sacrifice
As a result, this Agni-Hotram is a deed from the creators' paradise |3|

Because of the sacrifice, the gang of gods attained Dyu-lokam
So, they pushed away the Asuras with their creative wisdom
Because of sacrifice, even enemies become our best friends
So, remember that creativity moves only if sacrifice binds |4|

From the creative mind, one can see Lord Prajapati
From divine busyness, one can attain the truth of eternity
From the propulsion of creativity, life descended on this planet
Everything is created in the universe from pure creative buffet |5|

Before creation

Before creation, Hiranya Garbha was only a phenomenon
This pure potential form has been the actual lord since then
In the beginning, He bore this whole world in his golden womb
So, one has to dedicate their devotion before entering the entomb |1|

Our beloved Lord of Creation has immortal moulds
He certainly has uncountable eyes and divine pedals
The Lord surrounded everything from all directions
He exceeds everything with only good intentions |2|

Purusha

The Purna, the one who resides in the Puram, is called the creator
In the time line, like him, no one can find another gladiator
He is the supreme being, the one who is subtler than subtlety
Because of his gallantry, this world is complete without uppity |1|

Including the past, the present phenomenon resides in the creator
The occurrence of the future resides as a seed in this supreme editor
Along with the immortal principle, this Supreme Being is with everyone
Though he is everywhere, he is not comparable to anything or anyone |2|

The glory of creation is greater than the glory of local life
Inasmuch as this creation is just one pedal of supreme's rife
The Paraman nectar is a three-fold grater with luminance
So, he is the locals' friend and philosopher in this existence |3|

From the creator, this entire aggregation was generated
From his creativity, these gross bodies are actuated
The enhancement occurred after the expressions
He retained this creation along with his impressions |4|

The Yagnic beings generated various kinds of food for local beings
Along with they designed villages and lives by keeping feelings
The Paraman cultivated Ruk and Sama hymns for measurements
So, everyone should offer devotion for him by pushing bloody demons |5|

The definition of Paraman is interpreted with several shades of gratitude
Along with the face, his limbs are measured with magnificent magnitude
Vastness and bravery sprouted from his face and arms with a certain cause
Busyness and service grew from his thighs and legs without giving pause |6|

The opportunity, power were born from Paraman's navel and head
The earth and the cosmos were born out of his legs and ears' thread
When he is ready for creation, the wise will begin their sacrificial acts
The three seasons' flow, fuel, and oblation are there for their facts |7|

Perimeters

There are seven perimeters there for animates and inanimates
Twenty-one great elements were created for their sustainable stakes
The ocean, water, clouds, and four winds are the perimeters for creativity
Mahat, perceptions, Tanmatras, and elements are there for its productivity |1|

Yagna of wise

The wise ones designed their Yagnyams with pure sacrifice
Long before, they thought of Yagnyam as their effective device
This sacrificial Yagnyam became primary in their act of ritualness
So, they conceived creativity as a resultant of their factualness |1|

Earth

With his own creativity, Vishwa Karma built this great mother earth
Juice from flow and flow from juice occurred in the event of its birth
The creator of this world designed this system in pure local interest
So, creativity is housed in human beings without a pinch of contrast |1|

Path

The one who pushes aside the darkness is the self-illuminated one
This omniscient & omnipresent being is equipped with divine fun
So, if one comprehends this super being's non-local combat,
He will survive the death handed down by this local acrobat |1|

This Prajapati came out of the navel of that great ultimatum
Then he created a variety of genres by using rational datum
Through meditation, one can comprehend all this sanction
and he can recognise that every force is under his compassion |2|

Who is this scholarly person's Paraman?
Who is this true aspirant's Atman?
He is the creator, the one who is the giver of creativity from eternity
Thus, everyone should surrender to him, undoubtedly with ecstasy |3|

The luminosity of knowledge initially gains the incubation of the creator
Then, the creative personality gains this illumination from his true mentor
Therefore, everyone should consider the experiences of creative personalities
Then they can submit their perceptions to Mood for creative responsibilities|4|

Anasarca and auspiciousness are the wives of that great eternal creator
They wear these day and night to support the locals' creative character
Thus, with the Ashwins, the stars are illuminated by these supporters
These are all the true words of decor for local superlative creators' |5|

Who is the one who created this ultimatum with medium and least?
Who is the one that created this perfect world with the colourful beast?
Learn about that creator, who is having a relationship with this worldliness
Observe his operations carefully to open the door for creative curliness |6|

Movement of the World

Including our mother earth, all the worlds are moving in the creative space
In conjunction with water molecules, our earth is living in historical peace
This is utterly false to proclaim that only the earth was born with the sun god
But the truth is that the lord creates an infinite world and sustains it in his
pod |1|

This mother earth gives every kind of juice to those who follow Yama
Because she comes around the sun regularly by following the Niyama
Mother tries this because she wants to give a live demo for the local
So, one should feel like she is a mom because she cares for every syllable |2|

Only through cute observation may this Soma enter into one's awareness
But sometimes he may be struck in between because of inner bitterness
One should try hard to get this "soma's secretion" by doing true meditation
One should know that few creators became rich by realising this secretion |3|

Retainment

There is a self-illuminating aspect residing in our great sun
Because of this, he is retaining this world with the utmost fun
So, all planets roam around the Sun for their own sustenance
For this purpose, he never displaces radiance from mundaneness |1|

The air-dependent life always cherishes the Niyamas
Because of this deed, the world gets status in the Yamas
So, the Sun god nurtures this world always, without fail
For the sake of creators, the light shines even without mail |2|

With his friendly nature, the sun retains every world
Surprisingly, he pushes the darkness when he is thrilled
In many different ways, he controls all his dependents
With his eyes, he observes the creations with precedents |3|

The illumination and the illuminator

The earth is hanging because the truth is providing the report
The energy is maintained because the sun is providing support
Because of cosmic order, this great sun is functioning properly
This moon is moving because the sun is shining continuously |1|

Because of Soma, our sun god is still very strong
Because of the Moon, this Earth can never go wrong
Soma resides nearer to the star, most safely
Isha's radiance is gripping creativity very firmly |2|

Do you know who this being that moves despite being alone is?
Do you know which should be the medicine in the cold breeze?
Do you know which terrain is good for planting seeds for growth?
Oh man, this is our mother earth, because she obeys Paraman's truth |3|

Mathematics
Along with our algebra, the Paraman developed geometry
This math was expanded for the sake of the hymns' trajectory
This form of art is very appropriate to Vedic Jyotish Shastram
and also has its own appropriation in the domain of materialism |1|

This arithmetic is helpful for calculating the visible ingredients
This algebra is useful in determining the invisible convenients
These mathematical forms are explicit in the Mantras' denotation
These are two concepts that are implicit in Vedic proclamation |2|

The Vedas contain the ultimate meanings of our planet, Earth
The Yagnyas are the pivot point for the present cosmos' birth
These "Somas" are the horse power for creative subjectivity
One can attain excellence from Vox for its radical objectivity |3|

Prayer and Dedication
Oh Tejaswin, oh brave, oh paladin, oh lenient
Oh omnipotent, oh omniscient, oh omnipresent
Please grant me the knowledge of creativity
Please expedite my inner quality with certainty |1|

Please provide me with food and energy for the sake of Brahma Karma
Sanction the seeds of bravery to execute the earth and the sun's Dharma
When asked, he will sanction without a feud by considering the rules
When one moves in true essence, Brahman approves everything with tools |2|

Which one is supernal and an illuminator for light?
Which one moves farther when awareness is bright?
Oh man, this is the mind that moves in one's dreams' moulds
It is the one who calls for devotion from the awakened grounds |3|

With the spirit, the eyes, life span, hearing, speech,
illumination, felicity, Yagnya, Stuti, Yajuh, Ruk, Sama,
Bruhat, Rathantara, and divine, be competent in my sacrifice
If one asks truthfully, the Brahman will realise without thinking twice |4|

Yoga
Lord Savitru plays a very important role in this vast laudation
If one is conscious, he accepts offerings without preoccupation
So, the wise people conjoin their minds with Savitru without hesitation
And they keep their creativity and inner wit in Savitru with preparation |1|

The expedient god, Savitru, amplifies our minds very carefully
For the expansion of poetry, he will churn the fire methodically
He appoints the Agni to carry the oblations offered in sacramentation
He jaunts on the altar to offer creativity to the wise for realisation |2|

One should ask for the welfare of creative subjectivity
In the power of Yoga, one should actualize its objectivity
This wise one, Savitru, always resides in the Shree of the Creator
With a good mind, one can make him sit in the seat of a proprietor |3|

This God loves the creators, who are his true voters
With kindness, he enkindles voters' inner fire sensors
But the Lord observes the creativity that is under world welfare
With bliss, he completes one's task if one is consciously aware |4|

The sons of the supreme creator are sitting in divine seats
They intuitively understood eternal creativity at great heights
If one gives homage, they will take them to the lap of Paraman
Then the locals may get their creativity with the Para Brahman |5|

This wise person always stays in divine heat
Those meditators unite their Nadis with a beat
So, all these yogis are always immersed in divinal song
Hence, they will actualise creation easily with a big bang |6|

One should unite their nadis, then expand with true concentration
Then they should put their seeds in creative slits with proper attention
Because of the implicit gab, the result will bang soon without contraction
So, with these traits, the locals will become professionals without
superstition|7|

Twenty-eight materials were gifted for the locals' welfare by God
These are created for the sake of creative sacrifice by the Lord
Earning creativity with welfare is the order of the Yogic culture
This should be the purpose for the locals who are fond of a future |8|

One should give homage to God because he finishes our inner enemy
Everyone should obey the Lord because he gives every sort of alchemy
So, one should actualise him by understanding the meaning of Vedic Mantras
Then only anyone can realise the creativity, with the help of right-hand
Tantras|9|

The Upasanam is a powerful instrument for one's creative nature
This is the belief of every wise Yogi who practises Vedic culture

The one who listens to this may actualise creativity in peaceful form
One can even observe how these creators are blissfully calm |10|

Our lord, the Sun is the form of life in the Vedic sense
He is the nature of bliss for the Moon in its beautiful essence
Thus, the gross and subtle are nothing but the Lord Sun himself
So, the gross form of the creator is the bliss of his innermost self |11|

Sitting in a comfortable posture in privacy
Handling perceptions with extreme delicacy
Thinking about creativity is nothing but pure Upasanam
Surrendering Atman to the lord is the act of Nirvanam |12|

In continuous meditation, the devotion takes a special form
Because of this act, the grace of the lord descends on one's realm
By repeating this activity, creativity becomes handy to any person
Hence, this yogic trick is indicated with certainty in the Vedic version |13|

Great lord Ishan is the one who is never affected
by the world's toil, lust, deed, wish, or imagination
He is always free from bondage because he is Purushan
Due to his ultimate creation, he is always our sensation |14|

The opulence of creativity is far beyond comparison
The lordliness of this lies beyond any exaggeration
Everything that is beyond reason is available for creativity
Nothing can be comparable to the success of its rationality |15|

The transcendental knowledge that is flying in the exaggeration
is different from the informational nature of physical operation
This is always collective, and so is the seed of fundamental creativity
Whoever thrives in this will be referred to as the "creator of the locality" |16|

The one who is not affected by the passage of time
never have the aspects of either mortality or crime
He is Ishan, and he is the cause behind any kind of creation
Therefore, he is the Guru of Gurus without local projection |17|

The essence of Om-kara is the creator himself
The recite's relationship with it is bonafide itself
so that this creator is eternal, like an illumination
Hence, this radiance is the energy within creation |18|

The wise creator should jaap this Om-kaara with wit
By fusing himself, he should feel the meaning of it
One should meditate along with the Isha of Pranavam
By doing this, the Lord Isha himself shines upon him |19|

From the super Jaap obstacles to creativity will be loosened
From the proper Taap, the self-religious' view will be tightened
Therefore, one should keep his experience in the Om-kaara Jaap
and should keep his true self with a pure mind in his Taap |20|

Before opting for creation, one should be aware of the disruption
Otherwise, the creator has to confront bundles of obstruction
But, one can handle these by understanding their symptoms
And he can avoid the contents of Chit without paying a ransom |21|

The vision caused by disease, mass, dilution, and illusion
The platform that is born of blunders, habitude, and reference
These are the obstacles that cause disruptions in one's effort
But by inhibiting these, everyone can come out of discomfort |22|

Everyone should practise asceticism in life to overcome disruption
Then they should actualise unity with the Lord Brahman by negation
Then one should understand that true love is the flow of his creativity
And realise that the Brahman is not different than his witness, with clarity |23|

To come out of duality, the creator should understand the Vedic wit
For the sake of bliss, he should keep all his four feelings in his Chit
The sinner and the saint are nothing but the construction of one's own duality
Kindness, happiness, friendship, and scorn are the alternatives in
construtivity|24|

By giving dimension to the Prana, the Chit becomes stable
Doing inhalation and exhalation properly, one becomes humble
These actions can help anyone to achieve mental stability
Then one can immerse oneself in creativity with agility |25|

By practising the limbs of yoga, one may reduce their impurity
When the knowledge is improved, he may glow with luminosity
The eight limbs of yoga are especially helpful for any creation
Knowledge with rationality is the arrival of real accumulation |26|

Where the retention is, there the meditation is
Where the meditation is, there the creativity is

Tuning the self with the Lord Isha is one's true retention is
Understanding the vitality of subtlety is pure meditation is |27|

Who is the one who is wise, calm, earnest, tolerant, and rational
Who is the one surviving on almsgiving without being emotional
He is the one who lives nearer to the great Lord Ishan
He is the one who may get Moksham through Surya Devan |28|

Something of quality is residing in the village of Brahman
It is systematic with the lotus and space as an organisation
Everyone should find this and live with it in blissfulness
And one should understand that he is the lord himself, formless |29|

The omnipresent Lord resides cryptically inside all animals
He is the one who gives attributes and he lives within materials
He is the voice in everything because he is an omnipotent one
By moving as an omniscient, he is the witness form of everyone |30|

Liberation

In the Upasanam of Ishan, anyone can come out of tribulation
Science can be obtained by excusing the bad characterisation
The Atman may discover the progression through proper propulsion
Only then will this local Jivan be content with his own creation |1|

There are always tribulations if one is only continuing on the survival edge
But with the support of Vedic essence, one can come out of this ugly sludge
However, one has to give up the hatred instinct along with the fear of death
When one destroys these tribulations, he may receive the Kaivlyam birth |2|

With the Satt, the purity of intrinsic potential should become equal
The consciousness of one's life should bend towards rational sequel
Like this, if all sponsored traits are nullified, which are in potential waves
Only then may pure consciousness be infused with the true good news |3|

The one called Brahman, who is ruling this world for eternity
He is the one in a position to give total salvation from this locality
Oh man, giving the inner knots a divorce is the true salvation
These truths in the s can be seen with one's own observation |4|

Those who are liberated always praise the supreme Lord
So they bring about every wish and wonder for this world
Therefore, for sacrament, one should understand this maintenance
Thus, long ago, Prajapati revealed the secret of the locals' sustenance|5|

Which is their inside everything, is the Brahman, the immortal one
The Atman, which is the seat of Lord Prajapati, is the local portal one
Only through this portal can one attain the realm of Brahma Gnyanam
This is called the pure, true success of a local with his biochem |6|

Please follow the path which is eternal and rich in subtlety
Then, observe the Brahman from the inner eyes with certainty
The one who realised this was liberated from uncertainty
and continued his life with the utmost fidelity and felicity |7|

Who is the one who is the supreme being and is life for life?
Who is the one who is Paraman and the mind of every mind?
Please understand him with your wit and sane logically
Then you see, this suffering never bothers you insanically |8|

The one who sees the plurality of Brahman in the world
will be caught in the cycle of birth and death with the gnarled
Therefore, one should observe that this Brahman is in singular form
The one who has no match should be seen by the mind without scorn |9|

This Brahman is more splendent and subtle than space
He is free of birth and death, and he is at absolute peace
Hey, man, please understand this being through meditation
But be conscious about the path with suitable accumulation |10|

In physical embodiment, no one can find that supreme one
and he is not available in the form of substance to local ones
Because he flows differently in everything and in everyone
Oh man, he is none other than Ishan, who is working for fun|11|

The kinship with the Paraman is actual meaning of liberation
The friendship with the perception is the path to salvation
This will be advantageous to the person who is travelling with rife
The one who accepts this friendship may lead a wonderful life |12|

The Supreme Lord Ishan is the real big brother to the local one
So, the whole world moves by obeying that Lord without pun
The residence of that Lord is of the third kind in this universe
In his world, the wise one moves freely because of Vedic verse|13|

Ship

Finally, the Ashwins will transport the one who has realised the supreme
For this purpose, they will certainly come with the ship without a scream

They will come down on the one who offered good things in oblations
And they fly without touching the flow for the sake of the locals' salvation |1|

Doctor

Hey Ishan, please grant us grains and medicine in the proper form
Make water, the wind, and Agni our allies without causing any harm
Ishan will listen to these prayers if one transgresses his six enemy classes
One will receive good health if he executes meanings in Dharmic passes |1|

Rebirth

Oh Lord, when I am born, please grant me the eyes of Pranam
Please allow me to watch the rising sun with proper Gnyanam
Like this, sincerely ask God Ishan for this grant of perception
For this, please execute all your deeds without any distortion |1|

Please, Lord, give me life force from this mother earth
Give me radiance and a body from Adityan and Soman
Like this, sincerely ask god Ishan for help with your conditions
But you should wait for the grant without making complications |2|

Oh Lord, in my next birth, grant me a life span without grinding
Oh Lord, in that stake, give me sane attributes without binding
With this, sincerely ask the Lord Ishan for the soul in brilliance
He, the Lord, will consider all these things if you ask in silence |3|

Hey Lord, please grant me human form, which is truly auspicious
Let my mind understand Vedic science, which is really factious
But for this, one should dedicate his entire life to local welfare
And so it should be with true fidelity and devotional software |4|

Those who carry out their deeds on a Dharmic path
will get an auspicious body and mind in their rebirth
Hey man, these things will be granted according to one's way of life
However, selfish motives can push the person into a miserable life |5|

The one who understands all life meanings by wearing Dharmic socks
The one who lives his life according to the orders given by Vedic vox
Will be born in this world with a body filled with eternal wit
and enjoys everything under the sun by not touching shit |6|

There are two ways to enjoy the results of virtue and sin
There are doors such as scholar, wise, and normal inn

Actually, the world will vibrate depending on observance
According to fate, the Rutam moves without reluctance |7|

The fear of death resides as an instinct by birth in all lives
Because of past experience, this shatters the mind with hard vibes
Due to this, the wish to know about immortality will rise in mind
This wish is proof itself of the cycle of birth and death in every kind |8|

King

The eternal Lord Ishan is the king of this entire universe
Everything under this is his citizens' descended with a purpose
The order of the lord's kingdom is vast and pure bravery
The space in this is revered because it moves in his slavery |1|

Politics, teachings, and Dharma are the Gods' three assemblies
Every bit of local busyness should move with them, in gentleness
If you do these three things, then only you can survive happily
The one who practises truth may become a member of his assembly |2|

From power and success comes an anointment for the king
He can then pair the brilliance with the charismatic string
This king may give the Ashwin Gods to one of his cultivators
He may arrange things for the one who obeys his orders |3|

Our omnipotent Lord is none other than the King of kings
He is the president of the assemblies of the world of things
He is the commandant of various kinds of local prosperity
But, to understand all this, one needs the grace of divinity |4|

The pelf represents his head, and success represents his face
The sheen is like his hair, and the kings are like his life force
Like this, the Lord wears all these limbs for his citizens
He is the emperor of felicity and salvation in these pentagons |5|

Every ounce of strength and stamina are the Lords' arms
Every piece of pure and true information is in his hands
For local custom, the retention of bravery is the lord's deed
His valour, fortitude, and potency are his soul in this world |6|

The nations are nothing but the great lords' hunkers
All the armies and all the lexicons are his local bunkers
The deed which gives the purest actual meaning is his fanny
For the sake of his children, he committed himself to canny |7|

The lord himself, flowing in both time and space
Because he is the source of all perception and reference
The Lord supports all kinds of lives, stuff, and Atmans
But he comes down only through unselfish Yagnyams |8|

This Lord owns the Lakshmi and Sarasatis' energy counters
Hence, he grants bliss and knowledge to creative promoters
Oh man, understand, he is the saviour in this world of wildness
So, please sense him implicitly with great dedicated humbleness |9|

The person who is rich in wisdom in the group of Vedic scholars is
The one who moves on knowledge along with good character is
Accept him and make him the president of your assemblies
because he is capable of shedding light on the local perils |10|

Hey, great Lord Ishan, always be the emperor of kindness
Please consider the good deeds of all of us with allocativeness
Hey man, pray like this because he is the one who will save us
Please don't depend on any worldliness because it is all fictitious |11|

Hey Indran, you are the one who preaches the truth with logic
You are the one who moves, as we heard, without trick or magic
So, please make me like you to advance in fundamental activities
And to defeat the evil that interferes with my sincere fidelities |12|

Oh Lord, please make my weapons sharp with robustness
Please make my strength stable to beat the enemy within us
After checking it's logic, make such a request to this great Lord
But remember, he won't listen if one is floating on a superficial board |13|

One should conduct war by taking shelter in the Dharmic form
One should lead his military by wearing a witness uniform
One should prepare soldiers according to their self-religiousness
For the sake of world welfare, one should keep his prowess |14|

One should follow Lord Indra, who is clever and fearless,
and Lord Maha Devan, who will compete for competition
in their war against internal as well as external enemies
If one prays with devotion, the victory is assured with Hermes |15|

Our great Lord is meek when he deals with good people
But he will be cruel at the same time to wicked people
Therefore, one should not lose one's balance in dualities
However, endurance is always a good thing in formalities |16|

A fighting attitude is important because it protects the efficient
This attitude will get an increment only if one becomes sentient
If one is able to develop this by considering the importance,
He may begin his own creativity without much disturbance |17|

The actual form of fighting spirit resides in the true Kshatiryas
The original form of delectation resides in real Brahmanas
One can see the same spirit flowing throughout the vastness
Hence, one can observe the Brahman in Kshatirya Dharmas |18|

The verve is the Kshatra and the potency is the Kshatriyan
As a result, the attributes of the lord sprout in Kshatriyan
Actually, a legitimate kingdom will denote factual verve
The mixture of power and bravery will uplift brave's nerve |19|

Kshatriyan should enhance himself to become the president of the kingdom
Kshatriyan should magnify himself to protect his citizens without boredom
Kshatriyan should rely on himself to rule the world under Dharmic clues
He should understand that these things are not free in this world of blues |20|

When the Kshatra Dharma is in the hands of Brahman
when the wise people move by obeying the Paraman
the kingdom will move smoothly with great prosperity
Then the brave soldiers will be born without atrocity |21|

One should select a brave, wise man as their leader
And he should be able to obey the great lord's order
Then he will take care of the kingdom without distortion
As a result, everyone can witness their radical creation |22|

Only the good heart is able to turn anyone into a sentient being
Only an efficient mind is able to look for that supreme being
However, only a good deed can instil these qualities in one
Because they have the strongest ties to the great Lord Ishan |23|

The person with Kshatra in Brahmanyam is able to win wars
He may discover the realms because he is able to cross all the bars
Every ordinary being should select the great as their true leader
Then they can stay in peace without climbing a suffering ladder |24|

The brave one, Kshatriyan, always moves with the glory
Because of his enthusiasm, he will mine the weapons quarry
Therefore, he is able to build the kingdom for the locals' sake
And because he is on high alert, he is never afraid of evil's fakes |25|

Prosperity is the true material for any country
It is the heart of the kingdom, but not as a gentry
Weal is nothing but the felicity of one's kingdom
All these can be earned by the king if he has wisdom |26|

Varna-Ashrama

All human beings from birth are only one kind
They can be classified as bad or good, as per their mind
The two groups can also be labelled as foolish and wise
One can observe these divisions measurement wise |1|

Which one is appropriate for everyone to adopt
Which one explains the actions in their proper context
That is the Varna Ashrama, designed by the Vedic scientists
It describes the powers because this passed the hard tests|2|

The Upasanam of Ishan, along with Vedic Mantras, is Brahmanyam
The perception is Kshatram, and this Kshatram is called Kshatriyam
The one who moves in virtues is denoted as Brahmin
The one who shows bravery in war is called a Kshatriyan |3|

According to Vedic science, there are four ashrams for local beings
There are Brahmacharya, Gruhasta, Vanaprastha, and Sanyasas with means
These are the four aspects designed for the locals to walk without faking
Dharma, Artha, Kama, and Moksha are there for them to walk without
shaking|4|

The Acharyan will keep Brahmacharian, because he is in gloom
To nourish him, he will keep him for three nights in his womb
The wise come to see this Brahmacharian after his second birth
Because the Brahmacharian took humanity for what it was worth |5|

This Brahmacharian expands the earth and space through his actions
He completes the world with motivation through his sacrificial functions
By giving momentum to everything, Brahmacharian completes the task
So, the locals will worship him without hiding their faces behind the mask |6|

The Brahmacharian is the most well-known from long ago.
He is so eminent because he is never blown up by ego
This well-known senior is always living in a state of hale
So, the wise will always seek him out without fail |7|

This Brahmacharian is always illuminated by knowledge and penance
By wearing the animal skin, he will go to collect the Diksha's ordnance
He will enter Gruhasta Ashrma after the implementation of Dharma
He will start to preach the knowledge after completing his Karma |8|

This Brahmacharian will publish the science of Vedic Mantras
And then, he will evince the Lord Brahman without the Tantras
Because he has true expertise in the eternal Moksha Vidyas
And he had long since refuted the demon's heinous terms |9|

The king should live like that great Brahmacharian
He should rule his entire kingdom as a true Aryan
He should provide justice without a pinch of evilness
With good deeds, he will become an Acharyan with politeness |10|

The Brahmacharian should overcome the opposite with virtues
Only then will he become Gruhastan in order to fulfil his values
But she, the damsel, should have a taste for radical creativity
Then they can lead their lives in concord with their objectivity |11|

The wise one breaks the worldly cycles to attain liberation
by moving themselves in observance of Brahman,
in Taapam and Dharmam, with pure devotion
So, one should know that only knowledge brings salvation |12|

One should remove their sin born of action
in body, in mind, in dreams, in perception
One should know that there is a coelom
to execute this in their Grihastha Ashram |13|

Acharyan should publicise the virtues with exaction
Acharyan should cherish society with benefaction
He should work for people by putting in an effort
Then everyone can grow in true Dharmic escort |14|

The Vanaprastha Ashram is to give true rest to the Atman
Its real goal is to realise the truth about eternal Paraman
For the sake of this, one has to find solitude with an attitude
But one can actualise these by practising pure gratitude |15|

One should earn Vanaprastham by completing his responsibilities
One should get renunciation after coming out of local disability
The sprouting of Quietism is the proper time to take Sanyasam
The Parivrajakam is a prime indication of Sanyasis' true sum |16|

There is a will in Sanyasis to know the Brahman through Vedic science
They will work hard to make Tapas a reality through Yagnic means
For the sake of this, they move into utter silence in solitude nodes
And they will try to understand the eternal pure conscious modes |17|

A true Sanyasis will never be interested in progeny
Rather, they are interested in obtaining consistent alimony
So, they don't want to touch the local prosecution
Instead, they desire to live their lives for divine procreation |18|

A true Sanyasi will reject every kind of inner desires
So, he rejects thoughts of prosperity and prestige issues
But he has tasted the actualisation of eternal Paraman
So, he loves to help the needy ones like Dharmatman |19|

Every true Sanyasi lives with greater responsibilities
Their true local acts are divided into five major categories
Including Agni Hotram, there are yagnays that are must-haves for them
So, they treat the Brahman, Devan, Pitru, and Athiti in his Upasanam |20|

The one who has purity inside will wear this world
He lives for welfare of the world without hot and cold
So, everyone should treat well this one with greater respect
Oh man, he is Sanyasi, the one who moves in selfless acts |21|

Great Yagnyas

Brahma Yagnam is the first one in the line of sacrifice
Studying and teaching the Vedas is necessary without spice
Sanyasis has to study the limbs of Veda for this yagnam
And understanding Ishan is important in his upasanam |1|

Sanyasi should use this great Agni to help his brother
He should illuminate Agni with his knowledge of power
By using the proper material, he should give the oblations
This is Deva Yagnyam for him in his local obligations |2|

The libation is the satisfaction gained by the deed
The Shradham is the service with the devotional feed
This sacrifice, in Vedic order, is the Pitru Yagnam
This is the most important virtue in one's sanyasam |3|

The Bali-Vaishya Yagnyam is an important Vedic order
So, everyone has to give oblation daily in a good manner

Offering to physical Agni by giving food is a Vaishyas' sacrifice
Helping each other is the true meaning of sacrificial dice |4|

Determinate
There are many scriptures written by enlightened people
They proclaimed the truth without any ugly steeples
So, this is self-evident because of the absence of partiality
Hence, these are useful in timelines because of their vitality |1|

The texts, which were written in the wise courts,
The scripts, which are narrated with Vedic quotes,
They are called the determinants in the land of wits
One can observe the proof of this in Mimamsic skits |2|

Just as our earth receives light from the sun,
these Vedic mantras touch the hearts of everyone
Hence, these are the real deals in the knowledge gland
This, in turn, illuminates the other glands of every land |3|

The postills of Vedic Mantrans are themselves determinants
The commentaries, which help the codes, are determinants
Much of ancient literature is a living example of this
One can observe the proofs in Itareya, etc., for this |4|

There are four branches in our Vedic sub-system
Ayur, Dhanur, Gandharva, Atharva are its words of wisdom
These will illustrate the application of Vedic Mantra
So, these are the self-evident rules for practising Tantra |5|

prelims There are a few branches in our Vedic limbic system
This will clear the doubts of the one who follows for wisdom
Mimamsa, Vaisheshika, Nyaya, Yoga, and Sankhya are the limbs
Anyone can use these tools to put their wits to the test in prelims |6|

If one studies fiducial scripts, he may be enlightened by knowledge
By performing his true functions, he may come out of bondage
One may become wise in his endeavours as a result of these two acts
But keep in mind that he should never run on flimsy facts |7|

Daiva Asura War
The savant is Daivam, and the fool is an Asuran
Sportsmanship is Daivam and selfishness is Asuran

The war between the truth and lies is the actual friction
The friction between knowledge and action is its indication |1|

Gaya Shradham

The meaning of Gaya is Pranam, and Pranam is Balam
This Balam is greater in Ojasvim compared to Satyam
The Gayatri is the true Balam of the protection of Gaya
The Gaya Shradham is actually the Upasanam of Prana |1|

The housework and elderly service is the Gaya Shradham
The study and teaching of Vedic Mantras is the Gaya Shradham
Coexisting with the helping attitude is Upasanam in Gaya Shradham
The actual way to get that Vishnu Padam is through Gaya Shradham |2|

Tirtham

Which one separates grief from every walk of life,
which one is a ceremony that brings purity with rife,
is the Tirtham, and it should be understood by everyone
So, without any feuds and violence, this should be done |1|

The father, mother, and the Acharyan are the forms of Tirtham
Education, Brahmacharyam, and Upasanam are the tirtham
The one who is in Pranam and Vedam has the forms of Tirtham
According to Yejur-Vedam, the preacher of truth is Rudra Rupam |2|

Naadi

The Naadis are denoted by the names of Ganga, etc.
Through this, the Sadhakas will do Upasanam, etc.
By practising this, one can overcome their own dualities
Retainment is possible for one, through its functionalities |1|

Pratima

In Vedic measurement, the duration of a year is called "Pratima"
According to measurement, forty-eight minutes is called "Ghatika"
The wise will perform their own Upasanam in these dimensions
And it is through this that he will obtain progeny without pretensions |1|

Planet Worship

In reality, worship of the great god, the Sun, is an attraction
Worship of the Moon is anointing the king in a kingdom
Worshiping Mars is all about dominating momentum
The Worship of Mercury is to form an alliance with Wise's agendum |1|

In reality, worship of the Lord Prajapati is to attract money
Worship of Venus is to receive food with a drink of honey
Worshiping Saturn is to earn wellbeing for one's own felicities
The Worship of Rahu is to actualise Lord Paraman's realities |2|

By worshipping Ketu, one may earn functional knowledge
Because of this, one can truly come out of their local bondage
Ketu will sanction everything for the one who is Dharmatman
This is only the path to awakening the true purpose of Jivatman |3|

Authority
Any rational person can learn and realise Vedic hymns
Because no kind of disqualification is there for local Sims
Vedic science is the illuminator of truth for the local self
So is eternal, because it is designed by the Lord himself |1|

Vedic knowledge is there for the vantage of local wit
The knowledge of wit is there to keep all local minds fit
These types explain the behaviour of human society
Remember, only by understanding can one cross mortality |2|

With the right attitude, one can become better and better
Otherwise, he may be trapped in an embarrassing gutter
It is sure that only attitude will define one's destiny with the path
But remember, wrong-doers have to face Lord Vishnu's wrath |3|

Study and Teaching
Every guru should teach all the properties of pronunciation
Every creator should learn this with Swara's punctuation
In the act of creativity, these things will play an important role
As an example, one can see what happened with the pothole |1|

The creator should have good and appropriate listening skills
With an oration, attention, concentration, and factual stills
In education, there should be a space for factual meaning
Only then can one achieve through the process of cleaning |2|

Inside that creator, there is a true, sensible, wise man
Including the Sun, there are many kinds of world clan
One should understand this great creator through Vedic literature
Otherwise, every bit of knowledge just bonds the local structure |3|

Veda is the non-local science behind every kind of knowledge
From this truth, one can get solvency from intellectual bondage
Remember, just from local science, one can never get actual wit
One may get a logical fit, but he has to move with a bondage kit |4|

"Ganaa Naam Tvaa Gana Patim Havaamahe"
This Mantram reveals the true nature of Lord Paraman
By practising this, one may come out of internal disease
Because, for Muladhara chakram, it will blow a cold breeze |5|

Easement

The wise people divided the eternal divine music into four parts
So, Druta, Madhyama, and Vilambit became local resorts
The fourth division is manifested by adding all these varieties
From this, wise people downloaded the songs of eternities |1|

Ruk-hymns illuminate the properties of the ingredient world
Yajur-hymns suggest perceiving things via functional mould
Sama-Ganam narrates the heights of the blissfulness of wisdom
Atharva-Tantric answers one's doubts about the local skepticism |2|

Along with Asthakam, Mandalam, Adhyatam, Shatka,
Suktam, Kandam, Vargam, Dashati, Trika, Prapathakam,
Anuvakam knowledge is there to teach and to learn
All these things will help to get away from lunatic burn |3|

To understand the divine love, Rug-Vedam will be helpful
For divinal accomplishment, Yajur-Vedam will be helpful
Sama-Vedam is a tool to earn the eternal tasty fruits
However, Atharva-Vedam can be used to fix internal nuts |4|

The basic element of Rutam is in the form of prayer
The consolidation of offerings resides in the Yajur layer
The elements of Sama totally talk about solace fashion
Atharva prohibits the movement of the dubitation function |5|

The one who explains the meaning of Mantram is called a Sage
The Gods of the Mantram will explain the local ingredient gauge
Chandus in the Mantram is there to hold the energy of Tantram
The tunes like Shadja are there for the pronunciation of Mantram |6|

The Niruktam scripture will offer the proper results of the vox
These outcomes will provide tendencies that are not a hoax

One should use this to read between the lines of mantrams
The sages designed this for the locals' heart sanctums |7|

What has a narration with multiple true meanings
What has notifications for functional elements?
It is known as the Niruktam, and it explains various contexts
All of this, however, highlights the singular noun as an asset |8|

Including momentum, there are many descriptions in Vedic hymns
These are written to have a friendship with educational monuments
These momentums describe the interactions with physical entities
Its architecture is an important tool to overcome local calamities |9|

Every kind of garment is offered by that eternal Vayu God
He acts as a perception to grasp the properties of the Lord
To support the forms, he moves through our earth sanctum
He will take an architectural bath in it to help the momentum |10|

Every life can perceive Lord Indran through opulence
But for opulence, one has to pass through God's surveillance
However, he comes after both momentum and movement
One can get true skills and art through that lord's inducement |11|

The Ashwin of Vedic voyage science is of the fourth kind
Including Ishan, there are active powers that are mentioned
The voyage is made up of many ingredients, including earth
In Rigveda, the architecture of this is described as having worth |12|

In preaching, Goddess Saraswati is the fifth kind, as per Vedic words
She has the support of Ishan along with many powerful words
This Goddess Sarawati is none other than the voice of Lord Ishan
Human beings should understand Goddess' actualities with passion |13|

With the support of postills, one can understand the truth better
This scientific genre will undoubtedly bring sufficiency sooner
Hey man, please try to understand Ishan with the help of Vedic limbs
His postills are the phenomena that will help to remove illusionary skins |14|

All this toil of words will have the same meaning at the end
So, they will feed the knowledge to a local intellectual mind
In an actual sense, these Vedic mantras are in the form of gnome
Thus, it will create the platform to realise these cosmic game |15|

Otherworldly nature can be understood through words in the world
The exercise of Ishan will help everyone to explore their inner world
From these techniques, one can learn the meaning of education |16|

Exercise

The speciality of words' worth is explained in Niruktam
Many kinds of this are narrated in the Rig-Vedic Mantram
All indirect arguments are maintained by the inflection of nouns
The direct ones are maintained by the Madhyama Purushans |1|

All Vedic mantras manifest three levels of meaning
So, one can understand its spiritual aspect with true holding
The realities flowing from the verb are adjoined by the pronouns
So, this will present all kinds of visible and non-visible gowns |2|

Prathama Purushan tells us about mine, including others
Madhyama Purushan tells us about you, including yours
Uttama Purushan tells us about me, including we are
For praise and the praisers, these exercises are there |3|

There is an exercise of Pratham Purushan for inert things
including the usage of Madhyama Purushan for spirit strings
For the sake of worldly as well as Vedic words, the rules are there
The goal is to get a bounty for the one who crosses the intellect bar |4|

Tunes

There are seven kinds of Swaras residing in Vedic Mantras
One can compose divine music by using fourteen Tantras
The Local can bring these to life in the realm of his inner radiance
Ayama, Daruna, and Anutva kinds may give them the higher glance |1|

One may use Ayama kind to prevent one's own limbs
He may use Daruna to bring in rough and upper swims
In making the voice smaller, Anutva will be helpful
By following the rules, the Udatta will be graceful |2|

Anvava-Sarga, Mardava, and Urutva are the lower notes
Shithila, Komala, and Signatava are the higher notes
All these are the supporters of pronunciation of words
These will enable one to spell the hymns in the proper chords |3|

One should spell the mantras with the help of three Swara pipes
One should recite hymns in a sense with the help of A-to-Ou types

Because all Swaras are in Udatta, Anudatta and Swarita manner
And one needs to place the letters according to Vedic grammar |4|

In Vedic science, seven kinds of Swaras are there
With the help of this, Mantram will glow with glare
To support this, there are seven kinds of division
These are the techniques derived from Rishi's vision |5|

Including Shadja, Rushabha, Gandhara, Madhyama,
There are Panchama, Dhaivata, and Nishada Swaras
The charm of these is narrated in the text of Gandharava Vedam
These are the basics for the eternal Gitam to attain divinal Nadam |6|

Grammar

All four kinds of Vedas will proceed with great grammar
One needs to learn this to go without their inner stammer
These proposed directions are subject to the Vedas as a whole
However, it never follows inflection simply because that has a role |1|

The main intent behind Vedic words is to convey true meaning
And each word is designed to convey more than one meaning
Here, all words lead one's mind to that Paraman's insurance
And one can see this signifier appears before Dhatu's occurrence |2|

The signifiers come in prior, after, and further places
Along with the prefix, the momentum comes as braces
All these signifiers are attached to every kind of action
Hence, these Vedic words are special in this cosmic fiction |3|

In script, there is a yoga in the usage of the fourth inflection
In this meaning, the sixth inflection comes in as an option
In the Brahmanic, writers used these with Rishis' permission
Hence, one can observe this grammar with a divine vision |4|

One should not consider Brahmanic scripts as having spiritual origins
And they should not change the meanings born of Chandus' sovereign
Sages found nine differences by comparing Vedic with Brahmanic texts
because, in the locals' minds, this could result in a dramatic twist |5|

With grammar, one can never touch the bottom of a word's ocean
Even with numerous births, no one can overcome this inner emotion
Therefore, great sages wrote many essays by diving into their minds
So one can find the purpose of words by keeping Sage's reminders |7|

One should understand the divisions of decor in Vedic grammar
One should learn Upama, Luptopma, Rupa, and Shlesha in a manner
These are used to decorate the Vedic subjects in poetic narration
But one may catch the true meaning by removing these fixations |8|

Chastity

That Lord is staying with the Sacred Radiant Intelligence Section
He will give food, including everything as a means of protection
This Godspeed is found in the manifestations of divine properties
He only designed this to check the strength of responsibilities |1|

That Lord holds all these worlds with the help of powerful verve
Because he is omnipotent, he will pour felicity into every nerve
However, blissfulness may not occur in the act of selfishness
but possible for the one who understands interconnectedness|2|

The nature of bliss is that it is possible for every creature
This treasure is a great tool to clean one's inner nature
But this will defeat the one who moves in utter iniquity
It will protect those who act with virtue and equanimity |3|

One should not worry because the Vedic vox is in a higher state
It will change their fate if they move with a high confidence rate
Because of mobility, repulsion may be generated in a person
However, one can progress with the grace of God's darshan |4|

Because the Lord is merciful, he will provide all kinds of life juice
He remains in a state of bliss with one who is closer as a spouse
However, without true cleanliness, one cannot experience him
But anyone can reach him if they lead their life with divine vim |5|

That great lord is omnipotent, and so he has a radiant version
Through communication, he will reach us as a brilliant person
Thus, God will give initiation when one understands his math
These words are born of movement on the eternal path|6|

Lord is the essence of cosmos and so he is the source of energy
He oxidizes one's wish who is trying to accomplish without lethargy
Blissfulness is the tool for the progression of Atman in this world
But one should understand that bliss is his grant in their field |7|

The one who is greatest is hidden in that latent voice
He is the Soman who gives momentum with a choice

One's requirements will be fulfilled as a matter of dedication
Virtue can be developed only when one asks with devotion |8|

The one who is radiant will influence one's heart and mind
If truly asked, he would provide food and shelter for that kind
It is really possible if one listens to the Lord's voice carefully
But it is only sensible if they follow his rules very truthfully |9|

Quiet souls never limit themselves to sharing their joy
These ones never hesitate to enter conferences to say hi
Because these people already understood the truth and a lie
So, they educate the people without charging a single pie |10|

Our Lord is pure and always pours happiness over our land
He wants to give success to the one who moves into Satt's band
To attend to God's concentration, one has to give up his local loads
Then one may receive his essence according to his inner deeds |11|

Our great eternal Lord always illuminates that divine lamplight
One may be able to see this through their intelligent insight
Oh man, the Lord is always ready to give everything to everyone
But he will check thoroughly before granting anything, sparing none |12|

The one who is strong can control his perceptions just by instruction
The one who is not lazy can move anything with greater construction
Oh man, pray for these qualities, though it sounds like selfishness
And understand that you can actualize your life by factual means |13|

Only with the help of bliss can one attain the divine probability
With adoptability, one can live their life with greater possibility
This knowledge cannot be obtained solely through macro investment
but can be accomplished by practising the inner micro assignment |14|

In attaining bliss, pure eternal knowledge is very essential
By the actual meaning of Vedic science, bliss becomes possible
If the states of consciousness are corrupted, one cannot attain this
But in purified knowledge, the local can attain that melodic bliss |15|

All normal beings are constantly fluctuating in volatile moods
But the special being is able to concentrate even on uneven roads
If one cannot stop his mind, concentration can never progress.
Only by understanding the divine can one come out of the abyss |16|

All pervading, our Lord is constantly engaged in action
He expects all local minds to grow to divine proportion
So, through Vedic vox, he expresses himself with divine vibes
He is sitting with open eyes to take all the burdens of the tribes|17|

Our great Lord is omniscient because he is immaculate
As an impresario, he destroys all the locals' ugly maculate
Oh man, understand. He passes only through spotless doors
He illuminates everyone only when they make good scores |18|

According to the measurement of internality, God comes in emotion
By giving happiness, he expresses himself in his glory as the ocean
But he will not move an inch if one's emotions are utterly nonsense
Actually, it is only by that lord's grace that one can feel divine presence |19|

The Sadhaka faces a great deal of hardship in his eternal attainment
By burning his body in Tapas, he will prepare his divine apartment
The one who is afraid to face hardship will never attain anything here
But the brave one will definitely receive the grace of God from there |20|

There is a great magical eternal strength in that lord's voice
Using this, a seeker can become more confident in their choice
But a seeker can progress only when he overcomes ignorance
And he may get a path after passing through a divine trance |21|

Our great Lord is naturally an inspirer of every good feeling
He will show a path for those who have little energy in their healing
If one is truly good, then the Lord will descend for their sake
So everybody should find a good path by not falling for the fake |22|

Our great Lord illuminates every local moving creature
He will touch the soul through the Vedic motive structure
But for this, one has to create humanitarian poetic deeds
For the sake of this, he created a stream of eternal words |23|

Our Lord will protect the one who will follow the true path
In addition, he will grant the ability to kill their own wrath
However, to gain this, one has to adopt God's great divine song
Then, by the grace of him, sanctity may flow in life for a long|24|

Our Lord pervades everything in the form of essence
He perceives the movements of life in the form of evidence
Thus, one should overcome their bad qualities as soon as possible
Then divine bliss may expand in their realm as a form of potential |25|

Our Lord is auspicious and hence cures every sadness
He's a good friend, so he takes everyone's condolences
One can oxidise their virtues by being friendly with the lord
By moving with momentum, one may get flashes from God |26|

Our great felicific Lord will grant a life span to everyone
In a friendship, he protects one with a reflective action
But for this, one has to move in the action of evolution
Divine power and technique can be gained by his affection |27|

By walking on a nonviolent path, one can get compassion
These premises can be revised, but only with determination
With a calm and settled mind, everyone can live in harmony
All these are designed to join in with the divine symphony |28|

He who is flying with blissfulness will enter into eloquence
He will continue to be pure by overcoming consequences
Sages used eloquence in Vedic scripts as a trouble-shooter
Because they gained this with the help of virtue's booster |29|

This wealth of eternal Vedas is in thousands of forms
It is well-paced and clean in manner, as per divine norms
That great Lord cleans everything, including one's intellect
And he ordered the locals to use these with clear prospect |30|

Every life in the cosmos evolves as per its own eligibilities
They resort to Karma in order to reap the desired fruits
The Lord is the only one who can provide appropriate results
So, every life begs him for eternity when it overcomes defaults |31|

The creator of this world is very radiant and too bright
So, he will preach at every moment with clarity of sight
But, one can experience God's voice only through insight
A seeker can then, of course, see him in broad daylight |32|

That Lord, in the essence form, always pours happiness
And he sprinkles every kind of fine juice with tenderness
The Lord moistens one's heart when they are truly happy
He will uphold one's life when they consume eternal sappy |33|

God, who is composed of the divine juice, resides in pure form
He will move quickly to the one who surfs in intelligence foam
God is ready to clean every life with the voice of Vedic Mantras
and ready to give anything to the one who has the best contracts |34|

God, who is brimming with divine juice, admires wise people
He will pour the happiness through speech, which is audible
God will blossom into life with describable qualities
Thus, one needs to love God beyond local quantities |35|

In this ultimate creation, our great God has no comparison
He moves for life, because he lives in bliss with compassion
This, however, cannot be experienced just by the use of intellect
However, one can find happiness in the realm of pure intelligence |36|

The one who is the inspirer of the world is the seer, the charmer
He who knows will receive God if he lives a life while wearing armour
This God provides the necessary vitality in the form of supplements
But, a great position has to be earned only through achievements |37|

Only this sadhaka who has attained the presence of God is good
He thinks of eternal truth and walks in non-violence as a hood
Only by giving up selfishness can one achieve eternal prospectus
This God will show himself to one who follows divine conspectus |38|

Through the vox, the purity will be overt in one's life
It helps to move towards perfection with little strife
So, one may gradually gain true science through Vedic hymns
Then he may establish an innate connection with the Paraman |39|

Oh, Supreme One, you are an admirable ultimate principle with true rife
And the basis for everything is that you are a pure part of everyone's life
Oh, man, the great Lord gives pure essence only in admirable qualification
He is the one who gives us a home in all ways, including with divinisation|40|

Our great awakened Lord is full of juice made of elixir
He is the one who can bring divinity into life as a fixer
By thinking in this way, anyone can grab this great opportunity
One may tear away the shackles of bondage if he has impunity |41|

That supreme principle is vast, the very essence of the world
That has all moving and non-moving things in a perfect mould
That descends on our world when righteousness declines
So, one must remember that's greatness with Vedic lines |42|

Our great Lord has preached the Vedas in his own voice
And he taught knowledge, deeds, and worship for one's joyce

With that, he has mentioned the importance of practising rightfulness
However, one has to accept this by questioning with prodigiousness |43|

Our Supreme Lord created every kind of local and non-local reality
And he will illuminate every mind by observing their true mentality
Like this, he alone is taking the days and nights forward without a break
So, through good virtues, one can luminate themselves without being a freak|44|

Our great Lord's sustaining power is very old
The parental force in him is very big fold
There is no place in this world where there is no such glory
One can understand all this by studying the Puranic story |45|

The one who is wise and good utters a sacred Vedic voice
So, they expand their knowledge according to karmic choice
The reason for this attitude is that God is residing within them
So, one should be attentive to his voice by avoiding mental sum |46|

One should recognise pure pleasures in proper karmas
One should go nearer to God by understanding alarms
As a result, it must be a constant call to every local soul
One should understand this to achieve a holistic whole |47|

Whoever ever turns towards life with great humanity
And strives for the progress of living things with sanity
For him, the great lord pours the juice of bliss, happily
Hence, they progress in life with divine vanity, agilely |48|

God is beyond everything in providing food and green
This Lord is also the cause of the world's being seen
God has great powers of containment and release
So, in good people, he is able to implant real peace |49|

Learning through the good flow of Vedic speech
By increasing intelligence in the senses' breach
These sages move towards perfection with virility
Total cleanliness is only a means of true ability |50|

One must conquer the deed and the senses to gain divine wealth
To feel the power of God, one should perform the feat in good health
Restraint arrest is beneficial for this type of eternal achievement
Locals are assured of this bliss in good deeds without disagreement |51|

God explains the feelings' actions under oxidation from the Vedas
He meets the pros with the bond of cleanliness born of Naadas
For the sake of evolution, our great lord creates great works of art
Along with internal revolution, he grants divine perks to the resort |52|

Through the Vedas, this God reveals the mind of the heart
He promotes desire, action, wit, and worship as forms of art
This Vedic Vox touches on Lord Vachaspati from every angle
In proper questioning, one's intellect touches him without dangle |53|

Wise people are capable of relishing the bliss of the divine
So they can show the divine to the ignorant as a bliss sign
Thus, if one moves towards him by measuring each step,
then all divine pleasure will be available at their doorstep |54|

God is in motion, so he settles everything with the help of emotion
He is the one who elevates the lives that are swimming in his ocean
So, one should understand that he is the one who leads the world
And he descends into one's heart, even though the local mind is whirled |55|

Our great supreme lord will never abandon local gentlemen
Because of one's virtue, he increases their age with adrenaline
He also fills life with speed because he wants to see one's evolution
For this to happen, one has to ask God for life with mind's revolution |56|

Only a vox full of knowledge can describe self-religiousness
Only a soulful voice can fill one's heart with blissfulness
So, let alone that this kind of bliss may always fill our minds
Then you see, your heart and mind will be loved by creative winds |57|

Every brave man must pick himself up on his own
The ten Pranas should motivate him in a positive tone
Thus, the forces can penetrate the target in the mist
But, before this, he has to get rid of bad things to assist |58|

From the four Vedas flows the stream of knowledge
One who attains this can bring sanctity without bondage
Such a holding power is ordained by only that lord
Anyone can attain this with an inner illuminative chord |59|

That great majesty is the cause of all the worldly flowers
When there is a reason, it will activate the divine powers
The Lord is the one who infuses this sense of progress
But we have to allow ourselves this light in utter solace |60|

Acknowledge, as our leader, that glory which gives orders
And please pray to God to form our attitudes without borders
Then see, he himself shows the way out of his great mercy
At that time, you can subdue the senses without controversy |61|

Objects exist only for the one who perceives their inner essence
Things are there for the one who belongs to God's pleasance
We must ask ourselves before indulging, "Is it really I'm ready?"
Life can be enjoyed only if you are eternally ready and steady |62|

The Lords' great and true devotees are ever merciful
They are also truthful, friendly, and truly non-sinful
Oh man, only these people are truly at ease in the world
Only such gentlemen shine, even in darkness with a hold |63|

These sane people move forward for soul purification
People with this wit follow their path after verification
These paths are meant to realise the real nature of God
To befriend such men, one should pray to that great Lord |64|

In pretentiousness, this man cannot understand Divine Gym
With an impure heart and mind, no one can penetrate him
Hence, everyone should first give up their futile actions
Then the Satt should be achieved by proper transactions |65|

This wise man must see the principles only in the context of reality
He must exalt himself through the Satt that provides him with fidelity
Achievement will come to him only if he is a clairvoyant
He can proceed only when the truth becomes significant |66|

A wise person should grow up among those who have knowledge
He should give up selfish feelings along with the local baggage
Self-motivation should be his main tool for inner aggregation
Smart work should be a stepping stone for his progression |67|

Gaining this Supreme Being is the success of any religiousness
Friendship with great principles is the objective of divineness
So, one should give up unnecessary things in differentiation
and should never mock the auspicious vows of integration |68|

The juice of bliss is to light the flame of intelligence itself
It gives joy to the wise because of its power to oneself
Such juice is to give space for revelation on a daily basis
Because of this, new energies arise in one's wit without crisis |69|

The all-pervading great lord destroys bad and evil deeds
He fills every local heart when one comes out of greed
Then he descends into the local mind and sanctifies it
But to walk in his path means making sacrifices by staying fit |70|

Through certain sacrifices, the living person gets prosperity
Additionally, these people will get protection from that integrity
The action of these lies in the seven potencies of the Vedas
One will get the benefits of the divine if he does pure Tapasyas |71|

When the experience of one who is full of juice is from the true form,
when one's disease-like qualities have moved away from his room,
our Supreme Lord descends from heaven into his heart and mind
In a way, this wealth is not only his but also the welfare of every kind |72|

A soul which is already immortal is not despised by him
That great lord will never cast him away from him
Hence, the order he gives has a good reason and intension
And he will come to you if you are under divine propulsion |73|

Greatness is truly putting everything out with enthusiasm
True knowledge comes from perfect divine metabolism
Even though this world is the land of the deed, it is terrible
Still, this world can be crossed by obeying the Mahat principle |74|

One should have a mature physicality to recognise divine power
And they should put aside their indulgence to climb the yogic tower
One should use yogic potential bravely for divine actualisation
However, if you only think of pleasure, you cannot attain realisation |75|

One's life should be attractive without getting caught up in contempt
An achiever should move quickly by abandoning lazy moments
First, the ability to advance must be earned by the accomplisher
Later pleasures must evolve by associating with that publisher |76|

The Lord of this world is very watchful and thus knows everything
He knows the movement of every mind by sitting inside as a king
Thus, one should think before allowing any emotion into the mind
And if there is Satt in our lives, the divine will surely blow the wind |77|

One should give up enmity and become a friend to all
For the abundance of wealth of all, one should set up a stall
One should equip this world only with their good deeds
One can attain God when they plant the divine seeds |78|

All these creations and their aspects are loved by all
Because this helps in spiritual upliftment without a fall
In this way, God is becoming the giver of everything to everyone
But divine light will move inside one when the right things are done |79|

All speeches should be dedicated to his glory
All life should be dedicated to Gods' category
All kinds of self-sacrifices are very dear to our Lord
Such glory should always be saluted with accord |80|

This eternal power of the Supreme Lord is incomparable
The righteous deeds we have received are also delectable
Our Lord can be recognised by this powerful Vedic voice
The brilliance that comes from this is a cause to rejoice |81|

Attaining God is the desire that gives eternal peace
He is able to wash out the evil mind in a fraction of pace
These qualities of great God should come down to us without fail
Fame that is conducive to progress is gained by receiving his mail |82|

Bliss will spring up in the mind because of the divine mellow qualities
Thus, God's presence is accessible to our senses in great quantities
His characteristic hymns are in the seven potentialities of the Vedas
If one does this, joy will spring up within a person in many ways |83|

God understands the feelings born out of the desire behind deeds
Thus, he always pours the juice of mercy on the good living creeds
God will give happiness and a good life by charging divine fees
So, for good deeds alone, strength has to be united with peace |84|

This bliss juice carries vitality in every stage of life
It also gives quickness in every move without strife
This juice of bliss pervades here and after life forever
Sharing such juice brings fulfilment as well as pleasure |85|

This bliss will bring the eternal flame of pure knowledge
Also, it brings wealth without causing collateral damage
Thus, one should make purity of his own through Vedic speech
Then, that divine fortune will come in torrents within your reach |86|

Our beloved lord allots the opportunity of immortality
Thus, he gives many births according to the deeds' legality
Therefore, movement must be gained in relation to his speech
Vedic light should be seen in everything along with divine reach |87|

Aranyakam

The speaker of the beautiful Vedic voice is everywhere
He bestows success upon the one who has a divine share
There must be merit to receive such a gift from the higher world
His all-pervading offering is the desire of the entire world |1|

O Lord, lift up the bond of knowledge coverage
Move down the desire for materialistic bondage
Please ask him to expand the bond of eternal feelings
To attain this, one must understand divine dealings |2|

Oh great Lord, please give me the eternal fruit of my deeds
Because of this, let me join you with some essential divine feeds
One should ask him to give this kind of opportunity to everyone
And eat the fruit with whatever essence you have, with divine fun |3|

This Supreme Lord looks after those who
sacrifice, those who lay down their lives
for truth, along with donors, wise, and scholar
Our lord always observes every divine caller |4|

Our Lord Mahadeva is well-known beyond all means
In reality, he is the embodiment of immortal scenes
Hence, Vedic hymns are to utter his name at every opportunity
So, one can reach him by using this knowledge with impunity |5|

In the herbs as well as in the creeper, divine Amrita flows
The flow of blood in Nadis interacts with the body, and life glows
It is the energy in inertness and is the current of communication
Hence, these are the precursors to life and the formula for evolution |6|

The wise man has the capacity to destroy darkness
A wise man helps others overcome any weakness
But, one should weigh the merits before consideration
Only then should the wise man's word be taken |7|

Our lord is present on both the Earth and the Sun
He communicates directly through words to everyone
The great lord gives essence, and he is the source of it
By exorcising demons, he allocates essence to staying fit |8|

Real enjoyment in life requires the things of this world
Thus, one has to strive for this too, with divine mould

These are to be won only by the most eternal prowess
And the spirit has to be maintained by powerful forces |9|

This god conducts a Yagnya, which is the universe's vibes
And he keeps the sun to preserve all kinds of local lives
As a result, the juice of life must be earned by him
One should rise to such a glorious mind by Vedic prelim |10|

God has produced medicine and a reservoir of water
He has expanded the air sphere even for divine haters
We should remember our great lord with calm gratitude
Darkness should be driven away using the sun's attitude |11|

The Lord is full of brilliance, so he is in the first place
So he is able to wear these bright worlds with his solace
Therefore, our lord is worshipped at all times by worlds
He illuminates good deeds in the appropriate divine molds |12|

This Lord who lifts up all never pushes down the fallen
So, He is always the goal for those who are crawling
No matter what trouble comes, one should move forward without fear
Sure, he comes down to those who work by making god as his dear |13|

The omniscient will flow as intelligence in the sciences
So, he will bring light to all kinds of local essences
Divine intelligence will eradicate evil in every walk of life
The essence's intellect will help to solve the local strife |14|

The knowledge and actions directed by God are followed by the wise
They listen attentively to what is said on purpose with divine device
Thus, his speech always carries eternal truth and actual meaning
So, we have to gain science from them with proper screening |15|

Our great lord gives movement to the macros as well as micros of nature.
He creates new names with the forms for the sake of worldly creature.
God constructs devices so that living beings may go on without deficiency
Thus, we have to know the glory of the Almighty with eternal proficiency |16|

He who is the controller of the universe gives us all movement
He provides all kinds of energy for the sake of self-improvement
There should be a sense of hope that this light has come to us
And therefore, the strength to walk with honour must be ours |17|

These semi-legs that revolve around the time wheel are beautiful
These changing seasons that come every year are really wonderful
Oh man, do you know this rain, wind, cold, and sun?
We should express gratitude for this miracle's fun |18|

Our great Lord transcends all the normal senses
So, he is always outside the grip of local defences
Our Lord is inside and outside the entire cosmos
And so, he will experience all kinds of life forces |19|

All kinds of creations together are only a quarter of that Lord
The rest is invisible to living senses and perceptional chords
With inertness and spirit, he is sitting, covering everything
Hence, we do not have the power to recognise his mainspring |20|

Because of God's mahima, all indulgences are brilliant
Because of his charisma, all our senses are intelligent
These observances within God's creation are miracles
For these great alms, one should understand his oracles |21|

The retention capacity we have is really brilliant
Our great Lord's Vedic voice is truly magnificent
If these should be abundantly fruitful for humanity,
One has to be able to suppress violence with sanity |22|

Vedic speech is pronounced with pure, clear sounds
By means of language, it expresses the divine bounds
This voice is meant to provide an evolutionary path
So, one can extend it in any direction with eternal faith |23|

Our great and beloved God preserves one's blissfulness
He protects the one who does good deeds from wickedness
God gives good things to the one who does good works
In this way, His glory will come forth with fireworks |24|

Our beloved God gives love without any reason
He shines from within to dispel the foul season
These divine principles are emanating from him
Hence, his principles will be restored with a hymn |25|

These local physical bonds of every reality bind the soul
Only godly relationships give freedom without much stroll
The non-local bindings of that effulgence are truly divine
These are pathways from the mundane to that great shrine |26|

Our beloved Lord, who creates purity, also removes sorrow
With clear vision, he grants indulgence from the divine burrow
This parentage is really for the essence of local life
He must be seen in the mind's eye for the afterlife |27|

The world's organiser is all-powerful and all-knowing
So he determines which world this life should be born in
Because he knows the whole world and its vastness
So, one should make a demand without any foolishness |28|

For any kind of local life, our great world is a twofold achievement
One is somatic upliftment, and the other is psychic advancement
Seven types of tools are always there for one's achievement
Life realisation can be seen by using these with divine agreement |29|

It is God who awakens bliss in the mind with divine flavours
He gives us things worth experiencing to gain eternal favours
One's attitude should be correct in order to acquire these
and should ask Him to inspire us to work for world peace |30|

A living being really needs the power of wealth
One should earn righteous dharma for his health
A man should be conscious so as not to stumble in his walk
Then the fortune of floating in bliss is attained without make |31|

The power of this god can be found in reverberating chants
That is, to give strength to the soul with potential words
Such a person is loyal and strong in the domain of values
But it is impossible to get it with the help of bad shoes|32|

No great fortune even counts in front of this great god
Even the brightness of the sun is like a lamp before the Lord
Follow the good path, thinking that you will get the essence
Who else can we really ask and take in without his presence? |33|

No world of this creation has the ability to win this great Lord
Because he has the power to remove bitterness from an accord
By pushing away ugly hatred, everyone should approach Him
Along with further decisions, everything should be left to him |34|

The Lord's greatness exceeds what is possible in this world
It is only in the spirit of alliance that he woos culture
The hatred culture in one's mind should be removed
If called by a pure mind, he will help you cross this world |35|

Our tools, which are given by God, are always perfect
In this way, he brings good to all in every aspect
Gifts given by God should be distributed to everyone with love
In this way, there must be a driving force that helps us rise above |36|

This life should dedicate its soul to that great Lord
One should try to gain bliss by removing the bad
This bliss alone is the way one can feel God's grace
If we have this specialty in us, we can find peace |37|

This radiant love should shine in the heart and eyes
Spiritual hunger should be quenched along with local ties
With motivation, one should move in the sense of manliness
Then strength and speed will be ours, along with godliness |38|

This life has to continue forever to achieve true welfare
Therefore, there should be progress in the mind's warfare
One has to ask himself about potential to see the truth
One has to find their way in life only in peace without Ruth |39|

Every moment, new creations take place in this reality
These earn progressive successes in local sensuality
Creativity has to be done responsibly and with affection
And wishes must have Satt in order to achieve evolution |40|

This God can be found only in the spirit of self-surrender
He who gives everything moves only after clearing every blunder
Thus, the true voice of these four Vedas has to reach our hearts
These desires of ours must be filled with the essence of the arts |41|

That great Lord permeates all the organs of each and every life
He can be seen only if we keep the essence in action without strife
In the flow of knowledge, the subtle and dormant should be known
It is only the feeling of love that makes life touch that great crown |42|

We should have good people who can dispel suffering
His words should clear the external and internal grunting
It is through their act that the living perceptions get protection
Then this bliss fills the states of life under his real motivation |43|

Suffering of mind and intellect should be kept in sportsmanship
To gain experience, be prepared to have conscience in relationships
Bliss is to be obtained from the contacts of the wise who have done so
These should be done with love, along with the family status quo |44|

Happiness and sorrow—more than either of them, one should gain bliss
The deep nature of bliss must be understood from the Vedas without miss
So, talk to someone who has truly attained all this action, practically
This contentment is what makes the darshan of the Lord fantastically |45|

This Lord Isha is the giver of life and the wearer of everything
In addition, he fills the body with the life energy of every being
He, our creator, is Most Merciful and cherishes us in every way
But he observes the good and bad who are standing in the bay |46|

Each and every force of creation is in that God's quiver
All these potentials are within the domain of that inquirer
We must ask Him for strength for the sake of a good world
Then he grants when one moves practically what Veda told |47|

This great cosmic order is made up of the greatest wisdom
If one understands the principles of it, it strengthens his system
Sanity and strength can be earned through this life's diligence
Cosmic order can be achieved if one has true inner intelligence |48|

Through this Vedic vox, one can achieve the welfare of all
Understanding Shastra can also lead to the welfare of all
Thus, one should know the hidden meaning of the words in the Vedas
It should be understood that it is a means of moving away from bias|49|

God is the master of both moving and non-moving things
He is the giver of strength to the senses of worldly beings
But these can never be earned just through indolence
An empty heart is useless and piles up great ignorance |50|

Disturbances in life are born as a result of deeds of the past
But the ability to face them comes with a deliberative cost
Desire, strength, and determination are needed to face this condition
However, these should be faced without getting into the wrong situation |51|

God, who destroys bad qualities, sees everything carefully
He has given motion to all things through love, peacefully
We have to get him on the basis of good deeds and moods
He is the benefactor of all life in truly good sacrificial seeds |52|

These beings should live their lives with ultimate sanity
One should strive for true knowledge through charity
These latent spirits must find success in consciousness
If this sensitivity is expressed, it will bring true happiness |53|

Misguided inner desires should be abandoned
Bad goals and evil desires should be removed
This weakness pushes people into really difficult situations
Thus, we have to gain strength through inner modulations |54|

One who sees comfort in the senses cannot rise in life
Restraint of the senses is the beauty of life without strife
Evolution takes place with pure knowledge and real wisdom
For this, science has to test the Vedas on a truthful platform |55|

The intelligence of God is worshipped for life's progression
It is the only possibility for life in the true sense of adoption
The purpose of this great Vedic vox is to ascend to divinity
If one follows worldly things, they will not gain prosperity |56|

He who gives food and so on will be worshipped in the world
He who gives growth to every life is the greatest in many fold
Without understanding this divinity, the truth cannot be known
One cannot evolve if he does not suppress the volatility of tone |57|

The one who speaks the truth never bows down to anyone
The one who truly walks in truth will support everyone
Any suffering in this world can be overcome by the truth
Thus, the Acharya walks the truth without being Ruth |58|

When restraint becomes accumulation, the heart beats
It creates energy in life that burns away every sin sheaths
This bliss springs from the essence of virtue thus born
These pleasures are a layer of cream on the heart's horn |59|

This God will never let the soul of life slip away
He gives the essence of Satt to all life in every way
Therefore, we should dedicate our lives and souls to Him
Should thank God, who gives strength with divine rhythm |60|

Our supreme God forms the causes for the sake of creation
And he gives all the necessary strength for local formation
So he shines in this cause within the heart, which is in captivity
Therefore, worldly things have to be put aside for creativity |61|

It is this supreme God who gives inspiration to local formation
He will never corner any living or non-living thing in frustration
He never wants these motivations that shine in people's hearts
But he asks permission for inspiration from constructed forts |62|

God will always provide what is needed for oxidation
He has filled the granary with rice, etc., for utilisation
This wealth has to be seen according to one's merit
One should follow cosmic rules strictly while using it |63|

This world is a land of indulgences that encourage restraints
These possibilities are yoga to overcome one's own constraints
So, life has to know the happenings narrated in Vedic lands
One has to use one's attributes to come out of worldly bonds |64|

That energy, which teaches co-elevation, obeys retention
It also demonstrates the same truth in one's meditation
What is worthy of singing should also be heard and sung daily
Which is worthy of praise should be churned in the mind, truly |65|

Those who live here with generosity appreciate a life full of light
They try to earn a living only in a way that the citizens appreciate
These are the pursuits of the world of life to gain the juices of bliss
It is a path for evolution under the control of the senses in an abyss |66|

Becoming should be in the sense of actually moving
A haunted mind must have the possibility of growing
One's inner faculties must help when they move on their own
Karma should be done properly when getting a divine boon |67|

Spirit gives rise to the principle of consciousness in its presence
It surely demands that one's faithfulness to Karma be in essence
This spirit is alert and diligently observes people's ugly laziness
This spirit comes to us only when we have pure and sure desires |68|

This Vedic hymn describes the juice of bliss in the form of evidence
This blissfulness engages life in the karmas in active divergence
There is no drought in this world for the elevation of these lives
If this is identified emotionally, evolution can be seen through vibes |69|

Bliss is born out of auspicious karma, which comes from consciousness
It bestows a pro-progressive capacity for local life in utter darkness
Only the truly wise can evolve using this pure and sure Vedic science
Only those who are aware consider this part of their divine alliance |70|

A clean and pure voice can earn a man's appreciation
This one can surely continue the flow of destruction
Such people are worthy of the supreme God's invitation
He can join the floating bank within the flood of creation |71|

No one should obstruct the path of true and pure merit
Hard work, devotion, and knowledge should deserve credit
One should proceed by observing the requirements of others
By doing this, life's problems will never spread their feathers |72|

What is obtained from food, etc., is always pure
This nature is truly sacred and provides cures
A minimum understanding is required to enjoy all these
However, one should not taint this with selfishness |73|

True brilliance can be achieved through the right deeds
Wealth can be acquired only through smart work precedes
This kind of bliss exists only in the essence of cosmic governance
This is attainable only through a life of sensual restraint utterance |74|

This local human body is truly an amazing structure
With body, mind and intellect, God gave life a mixture
It should be used to protect the universe's pure essence
This intellect has to be utilised for the welfare of existence |75|

A true feeling of friendship in an emanating formation should arise in us
The sensibility of any structure must be recognised in its perceptional status
This is the communication between the cosmic eminent and the local observer
Beyond Vaikhari, Madhyama, Pashyanti, Para modes of communication are there |76|

Brahma consciousness is the seat of true vibration
Shastra consciousness is the way to man's liberation
The Brahman of this domain is already present in all beings
One has to realise this element in their three conscious things |77|

Karma done in true bliss becomes complete
Thus, it increases the essence of life in the feat
Enemy qualities should be left behind for this pleasure
Evolution must be made real by these kinds of leisure |78|

The great God Aditya gives life to every local illustration
He fills the soul day and night with continued illumination
By using the Jyoti, he cherishes the fortunate in the world
In the guise of Gayatri and Savitri, He descends into the mould |79|

Willingness is a wonderful force that brings happiness
This is a great philosophy that removes any darkness

This one divine power that perpetuates good is for life
We can realise such a powerful role without much strife |80|

Jivas are alive because of the forces of air called prana and apana
These are the only possible means of completing the will of Jiva
It is only through the firmness of these blessings that resolutions are fulfilled
One has to move on the path of gaining elevation with a good character
build|81|

Those who follow the juice of bliss are fearless
Many people share knowledge to make progress
World affairs are conducted by such a pure soul
Anything, if used in a good way, can play a divine role |82|

This universe is happening because of the observation of consciousness
This flame of life is moving because of the energy of consciousness
This energy plays a role as a platform in this history of behaviour
This same consciousness is present in everything and everywhere |83|

Only the wise can understand this set of great qualities
With a pure mind, they will know the Supreme Beings
It is only through their teachings that our awareness increases
But if we procrastinate, we will never have these opportunities |84|

Lovers of blissfulness give direction only to those who seek progress
They develop those who walk the right path and instil pure coolness
Those who care for and share our local world always think of others
Lovers give energy to the senses because the world should progress |85|

There is no living being in this universe who does not desire bliss
There is no one in this world who can resist an exciting spirits
Those who are consistently engaged in karma can earn these
For the sake of evolution and inspiration, no one should miss this |86|

He who realises his true form transcends the three natures
He spreads the bliss to the worldly local living creatures
These great people will spread the truth through their actions
We should worship the feet of such people for their perfections |87|

Good karma should also be observed daily in our walks
One should remove tensions and progress to avoid shocks
This world does not exist only in the sense of experience
So, one must identify creativity without any annoyance |88|

All kinds of words have come from Vedic literature
It is the flow of holiness to the manifested creature
There is an applicable meaning hidden in this poetic voice
The actuality of this should be seen in Swa-Dharmic choice |89|

Vedic vox gives evolution and revolution with calm
The application of this leads to the realisation of who I am
This voice is the only bridge from the manifest to the un-manifest
Vedic Vox means a vehicle that completes one's local internal quest |90|

Vedic voice potential, along with energy, is very sharp
It is to beat the bad professions and tune the inner harp
If we are engaged in good deeds, then no evil will affect us
This bliss is very superior to every life of a local pileups |91|

One who moves in essence perceives truth from the Vedas
According to their merits, they gather the joy that is born within's
This kind of sacredness is always flowing in the same mode
One can also experience this if he ties his mind to the divine node |92|

The feel of witness in a structure is the sole ruler of this world forever
It shares everything without expecting anything from the local flower
But it does its work only according to inner and outer rules
Ideal men and gods will be born from these principle schools |93|

This witness plays a major role in all kinds of happenings
The principles of genius and scholarship are derived from this
The successes in the awareness of knowledge go beyond examples
Therefore, the witness should do business with knowledge models |94|

This witness is a true friend who is always without fuss
In every moment of one's local life, he is always with us
Witness only created this whole world with the realities
If you know this witness, you understand divine priorities |95|

The voice of this inner witness will not tolerate the evil route
Even though this voice seems harsh, it leads life on good feet
We have to understand its true voice with inner peace
This is the only way to be happy in this world of race |96|

Our inner five knowledge senses perceive brilliance
This will provide valuable wealth with utter tolerance
With its help, the structure can identify its witness
Because of this, life can be enhanced through fitness |97|

One's life is to be illuminated by enlightened willpowers
Knowledge should lead to the prosperity of the world's powers
Thus, potential as well as energy have to be filled in the senses
For this to happen, the witness must first be known by inner expenses |98|

One should not indulge in blundering while gaining strength
And we should keep pure consciousness within a wavelength
Happiness should only come from things that are good treat
Preserving what is gained without erasing it is really a great feat |99|

These charities, which the great Lord gives, are principles of bliss
These are great safeguards against destruction without miss
No matter how much is given, his wealth never diminishes
The full is never incomplete, no matter how much it is refinishes |100|

Compassionate beings leave the path of evil
They walk to get auspiciousness on their own will
Those who walk this way are closer to the witness form
They remove the evils with the power of the soul's norm |101|

Every life should give goodwill to everything in this world
One has to gain patience in the control of the senses in his mould
The form of witness in the depths must be heard
To attain divinity, one has to be patient like a flying bird |102|

Senses are there for the convenience of human life
There are ways to enrich, comfort, and indulge, to ripe
These types of energies exist in the world in different forms
To get these, one has to get strength from virtues in life norms |103|

There is witness in both manifested and un-manifested forms
Even everywhere, he is connected to conscious norms
He moves the universe through communication patterns
So we have to achieve the levels of awareness that Saturn's |104|

The life of a local sentient being must see development
Thus, they should attain the connection of the wise compartment
Purities should be known through the one who knows Brahman
All kinds of indulgences should be given to the life of a human |105|

There is longevity for the sentient in devotional sacrifices
All kinds of happiness exist only because we give up selfishness
Only one who is truly generous accomplishes great deeds
Only when he is radiant will he become resolute in the moulds |106|

According to energy, local sentient life will be born
Because of actual achievements, one will be worn
Our mother, Prakrity, is going on for those who have little energy
Creation is moving in the interdependence of Prakriti and life lethargy |107|

In this world, disruptions affect local life a lot by rolling in
To win by these means, one needs strength and perfection
All these disruptions are mainly due to inner ignorance
But one can overcome it with knowledge and tolerance |108|

Those who care about inner witness surely love pleasure
After thinking, they do deeds in the world with leasure
So they don't have physical, psychological, or energetic heat
They will motivate others to observe inner witness with a treat |109|

He who knows witness is able to swim in this sorrow and pleasure
He is able to save the truth in this flood with the purest leisure
He is the true and pure inspiration for all local lives forever
He alone is revered among all locals because of his endeavour |110|

The voice of a witness has the power to convey the truth
Thus, it has the passion to inspire local lives in pure faith
The inner evidence is the ultimate, if sought after properly
These knowledge and sciences end in witness's scholarly |111|

These scholars bow down to the voice of the Vedic mantras
They are inquisitive about the body's, speech's, mind's tantras
The mantras in this Rigveda speak of inner witness
This power of retention will come only from progress |112|

In Vedic vox, there is knowledge, karma, and worship fitness
An invocation from the Vedas conveys the true witness
All these Vedic mantras are also the yardsticks of truths
It is to gain Dharma, Artha, Kama, and Moksha's booths |113|

In order to realise supreme witness, life must become evidence
Sacrifice and good deeds should be done with diligence
Then the supreme witness gives verve with pure vision
Then humanity becomes the vision for the practitioner's religion |114|

Ultimate tolerance is the hallmark of that greatest holiness
The expanse of purity is the manifestation of divine greatness
Thus, purity should be attained in a cause that can be fulfilled quickly
One should observe this great brilliance moving within, frankly |115|

Those divine principles are propagated in the universe
That truth is ascertained from the hearts of great sages
The sages have generously shared the meaning with us
Such rays of knowledge should be carried with synthesis |116|

Eternal and true Vedic voices illuminate pure Gnyanam
They also dispel darkness along with the Agnyanam
If the voice is not held tightly, that light will not be generated
If evil careers are removed, only then will light be propagated |117|

The inner NADA pours out without making any noise
It is always equivalent to pouring out with divine choice
It is right at the edge of the lightning world inside
This is the only link to a supernatural connection outside |118|

There is wonderful joy in the testimony of great bliss
It shows the ascetic the joy of knowledge without miss
We must move forward with this eternal divine knowledge
Then the darkness of ignorance will be dispelled by its badge |119|

The flame of the inner soul flickers within a local being
It reverberates every day steadily with the sound of pouring
Hearing this, the cultivated bad professions will run away forever
There are no premises for this soul that can be known from outside,
whatsoever |120|

This evidence (the soul) is hidden in the heart of life
He shines into life, definitely only in the mind's thrife
He will manifest in the profound powers of penance
He shines in the worship of deeds with boastance |121|

The body of this eternal soul is temporary in manifestation
The great soul's body is only in the flow of actualization
Great knowledge resides in this local mortal's head
This knowledge has to be gained only in the divine's bud |122|

The divinal moon god reflects that great eternal sun's rays
In the same way, the witness within us reflects God in many ways
Thus, males and females have to recognise this witness forms
It is in him, that we should hear the bliss of loving norms |123|

This invincible elemental Supreme Lord is the Beloved of Every Life
He is always shining in the innermost being of the wise, without strife

He, who is thus dynamic, elevates every local life to a position
With the help of this, one can cross the barriers with an elevation |124|

There should be a leader who helps us overcome obstacles
That supreme alone should be the legislator to rule our practices
This soul, which is supremely brilliant, should be our leader
He should also be the lawgiver of this community's world order |125|

Chandus makes us drink the bliss found in Vedic's viscosity
Surely it gives us the inner strength to achieve tenacity
It is these Chandus that are the basis for the evolution of locals
It is a covering of protection in trans-birth, as seen in vocals |126|

Witnesses like that in life don't really move anywhere
But every minute, it keeps every local clan really alive
The soul is the conductor of energy, both macro and spiritual
He is supreme in power and in great splendour as a supernatural |127|

This testimony is bright and never forgets the livings
He preaches by creating a work for the earth's beings
Truth bears good fruit only if it abounds purely
Thus, the next generation should realise his need, surely |128|

These trade skills are really essential for all local forms
Essence without betrayal is sufficient for local norms
Only then will the generous give you good knowledges
Only by becoming wise can one earn fame and badges |129|

From birth, humans are full of the purity of the local and divine
They will be born on earth because of the essence of non-divine
Because of nature, they get busy with deeds of plurality
Hence, they should move from duality to divine maturity |130|

Local lives should be settled with strength and speed
One must be engaged in trying to gain a witness's deed
Its ray must be known because it is necessary for evolution
As a producer as well as a director, one should gain revolution |131|

One who does wear is described in one way or another
One who does wear is narrated as the greatest forever
He is all-seeing in the genius principle in one's locality
He has to be sought in lust with the help of divinity |132|

This life that is born, lives, and dies is itself proof that there is evidence
This variety of local structures is the success of eternal evidence
Brahman does penance, endures its heat, and creates life continuously
So, at least for himself, this human being has to do penance cautiously |133|

This supreme witness shines externally and internally
This great one takes knowledge from his womb cautiously
He is the one who favours the voice that sees progress continuously
Listening to this will definitely change our minds' careers, seriously |134|

This paraman weaves orders into the universe
Internal and external codes rule his multiverse
By observing these, Swa-Dharma will be understood
He is the witness within us all, with a cute livelihood |135|

There are obstacles and worries in the effort to progress
There are difficulties in the ways of Yaga and sacrifices
Therefore, one should keep their mind only on good deeds
The essence gathered in this way will show the good feeds |136|

These actions and deeds are sheltered by the soul itself, forever
Eternal knowledge has given us knowledge that He is our helper
He provides everything in good deeds and karmic facts
He punishes without pardon for every local's bad acts |137|

God is needed on Creation, Condition, and Dissolution's stage
He should be remembered in childhood, youth, and old age
Soma juice is secreted from our eternal paraman's essence
From this, lives can evolve in an instant in the divine presence |138|

Those who do not back down in conflict will find divine riches
He who conquers the mind and intellect attains heroism badges
With the help of the riches of heroism, local life becomes a field expert
He advances faster with the help of momentum without a neck-hurt |138|

Supreme glory has already created the necessary things
He is always alert for the protection of the decent ones
The awareness of sharing is the principle of the genius herd
It is wickedness to talk and gain by deception in this world |139|

Several vows of non-violence touch our Mother Earth
This nature gives health through elemental purity at birth
These mothers desire inner resolutions with true merit
Their satisfaction should be in mind while paying the debt |140|

Yagnyas prescribed by the Ruta are meant for elemental purification
It balances the external and internal in motion under notification
It is the pivot of eternal time that weighs right and wrong equally
Locals should not ignore God, who has done all these things meaningfully|141|

There is no end to the understanding of this evidence of the divine
He has no limits on imparting worldly and non-worldly design
So, from the milk of knowledge, ghee has to be curdled by deeds
And that ghee has to be sacrificed for the welfare of the worlds |142|

Great eternal omniscience has an over-pervasive power
It keeps the pace of the world as it was in the past to empower
The power of intelligence is to inform us of this great mystery
The brightness of the testimony will benefit the world through history |143|

One who has acquired firmness of mind understands Vedic hymns
They show good, useful things and residences for our local limbs
Therefore, practitioners should listen carefully to their words of warning
Tenacity must be acquired through the power of discovery every morning|144|

This world is to give credit to the natives by going nowhere
It is only from here that life and non-life have to go there
Locals should roam in order to get the fruits given by the trees in the nation
One has to reach there with a smile that shines with the power of
emotion|145|

Life should not become infatuated with a mere temporary body
This fascination should not affect us at the time of leaving the body
If God is thought of as everything, there will be no pain in death
If so, one can recognise evolution at the time of death and in rebirth |146|

It is this testimony that protects the baby in the mother's womb
It is he who performs the functions of the organs in rules mob
When mind and knowledge are united, you can perceive witnesses
Thus, the reason behind His mercy is that you may evolve with fitness |147|

One should earn by one's own efforts and expand what is little
Karma in goodness should be offered to the world of the brittle
Then the evidence will always come here for one who is righteous
This is the platform for punishing the wicked and protecting the virtuous |148|

Material acquisition is great for every person's local belts
The power to attain divinity is greater than anything else

The earning power of men and women is really high
Only in the flow of knowledge will the supreme grow high |149|

A wearer of senses can understand the demands of life in motion
They come to mind only when there is dedication and devotion
These senses are in everything other than divinal forbidden
He can be known through communication when good moves in |150|

Only with true patience can one find God in life's grind
He is accessible only to those who have a still mind
He is the Witness, and He has also seen into the heart
Thus, life should look at such glory with discernment's part |151|

An infant is born and grows because of testimony
Its life is continued by Guru and father-mother's matrimony
It becomes wise through the instruction of geniuses
It becomes man through the science taught in the Vedas |152|

Because of this genius quality, one gets the seat of this life
By thinking of the Purusha Yagnya, one moves without strife
This life becomes pure only if it produces progression
Because of inner purity, one can get divine protection |153|

Kind of hook-ups and breakups occur for human beings
Thus, the evidence appears to be far or near in feelings
But this fraction of eternal witness is in the hearts of humans
This should not be sought by getting caught up in emotions |154|

This evidence appears only on the basis of true knowledge
He comes to light in order among those who have wit's badge
He himself stands up as one who achieves true progress
For this reason, the senses should be controlled with firmness |155|

There are great beings who perceive the essence and the abstract
These humans use such power wisely to have divine contracts
They lead life with surprises to get that great lord's tweet
Therefore, one has to worship these people's lotus feet |156|

This eternal witness shows a clear goal for life's directive
He gives leadership to the self as well as to the collective
He is always the instigator of essence in any practitioner
Thus, witness expands the field of action for the missioners |157|

These rays of the sun inspire every local organism
These rays of knowledge expand the universe's system
There is a greater pure purpose in all these divine rays
Evolution is the main reason for this, along with the pace |158|

Local organisms can lead their senses with the help of truth
Deeds can be expanded along with the knowledge, in sooth
Thus, Varnashrama tempers the lives of local organisms
This essence of truth pours forth experience mechanisms |159|

This knowledge of the great supreme is primordial as well as immortal
Along with these things, organisms are born from this knowledge portal
Thus, life thoughts have to understand the science within it
Then awareness will be born with brilliance, and life will be hit |160|

These physical, mental, and energies are the wealth of organisms
Awakeness, dreams, and deep sleep are consciousness' mechanisms
The awareness of these consciousnesses is in three-dimension
Organism has to grasp these riches for its evolutionary mansion |161|

Towards a body clothed with good things,
With a voice that invites pure divine things,
Our Lord comes to human beings with a big bang
This care and nourishment is good for life's slang |162|

It is our great, supreme Lord who inspires us to live a mature life
He leads a dynamic one to a better state without much strife
Therefore, every internal deed should be dedicated to our Lord
The best of Vedic vox should be offered to him with divinal ward |163|

By non-violence, this God has placed in us that which wears Pranas
He has given the promise of protection if one is worthy through the Vedas
Therefore, one has to bear everything bravely and move forward
Violence should be eradicated by the flame of wit, which is inward |164|

These practitioners have been working hard for centuries
They received God's help in getting an education when in miseries
Only a sense of sportsmanship can remove the slyness' felling
Being very old, this ashram has never been weakened by kneeling |165|

In self-religiousness lies the truth, which bestows virtues
It contains a flame that removes evil spirits from non-virtues
It should be noted that self-religiousness is a torch for truth's game
Offerings should be given patiently to the one who is made of flame |166|

No one should commit sin by sitting on an ignorance' chair
No one should set his mind to deeds that do not bring welfare
We have to take care that these diseases do not overwhelm the mind
We should proceed by maintaining proper paranormal levels' kind |167|

The Yagnya performed by the couple should be proper, in truth
Non-violence should lead to growth in divine qualities' booth
Only then will a son be born who observes the Vedic speech
Seven generations will gain salvation through his Vedic reach |168|

It should be known that the wise man was born of sacrifice
And this man is moving in the brilliance of cosmic' dice
It should be known that these Vedic teachers have taken the wealth of God
It should be seen that the wise man is speaking the language of the Lord |169|

Publishers tend to knock off bad works of bloody moods
They fill the world with the deep essence of proper deeds
By doing good deeds, they bring down normal parallel growth
With increment, they also take us with them as their oath |170|

Divine ability puts everything into probability form
Divine deeds alone make life a possible norm
In this world, manifestation from the potential is taking place
So one has to allow this in his pure and true thought's brace |171|

There are three destinations for life
It is as unique as Dyu, earth, and space
All three worlds can be worn by adopting principles
One can realise these through the karma of physicals |172|

Purity cannot be defiled by acts of violence
The complete can never be defeated by force
Because potential is behind all qualities' lumps
Will the great-lord sun be lit by a lamps? |173|

That potential is very strong with all powers
It destroys ignorance as well as evil forces
It is this potential that swallows up everything in the destruction
In fact, the same leads to all kinds of work, including fiction |174|

The vox of the Vedas will be revealed in the destruction of bad careers
A good history of life will make brilliance shine by crossing barriers
This is the path of evolution on which one should advance
This blissful state is the direct path, without any chance |175|

These Vedic voices always bring to light only the sacred
It will become an experience when the shackles are removed
This loss and gain is a warning sign for life's flow
If you know this, you will get riches without a blow |176|

The energy gained from true knowledge dispels darkness
It lights the flame and imparts knowledge that is flawless
This world is running according to those divine rules
Life is not beyond this, meaning day and nights' flow |177|

These consciousnesses of various kinds are born only in dynamism
They understand the Vedic language as per their own mechanism
Thus, consciousness creates various paths for attainment
But these methods reach potential at the end of detachment |178|

This potential will work for the one who overcomes the senses
Desires will be fulfilled for him just by being willing fences
All that is created is under that great Paraman's control
He melts only for the local and non-local efforts' patrol |179|

Song

Gana Vidya is one of the eighteen Vidyas of Vedic origin
Along with Sama, there is a type called local stores in
The body of potential is the instrument for Sama Gaana
These instruments of stringed ones are called local Gaana |1|

Krista, etc. are the seven vowels of Sama's ascent
Shadja, etc. are the seven vowels of Sama's descent
This Sama Veda is the true source of musicology
Gandharva, the sub-Veda, is the music's semiology |2|

There are voice variations like mrudu, madhya, ayata, deepta and karuna
There are these hymns of Savana in manda, madhyam and taragati
The Song form of Udgatri is to begin with Sama singer splice
Veena has to be initiated by singing in the music sacrifice |3|

The fulfilment of any karma lies in ending it with the song of God
According to the Saama Veda, there is surrender to that Lord
It is the Saama that is to establish that I am yours, wholeheartedly
Mandra on Veena is to play Saama softly and solemnly |4|

One of the particles that are in the sun's rays is called a sound molecule
When it enters the heart, it actually becomes two molecules

When the same tip of the nose is touched, it becomes three molecules
When it touches the tip of the tongue, it becomes four molecules |5|

The movement of molecules is a calculation of time called maatras
Its calculations are made from the cries of birds' sutras
A crow's cry is a long one, while the chausha is a short vowel
The peacock's call is Pluta, and the long syllables compound the Vriddha
vowel|6|

The effort to do so in a particular position is the emergence of sounds
The touch made in the upper part of the throat is Ucchairudaatta
The touch at the lower part of the throat is called Niichairudaatta
and the mixture of these is called Swarita, according to Vedaanta |7|

Only when this prana air takes place from
the nose, throat, chest, mouth, and tongue
and including teeth, the seven tones are born
The time taken in this process is said to be Matra |8|

When air touches the head through the navel, it becomes Rishabha
Gandhara swaram in the nose, Madhyam swaram in the heart
It becomes panchama in air, chest, heart, throat, and head positions
When all the swaras go away, it becomes the Nishadha swaram |9|

Samadhi

These normal parallels in humans are powerfully rooted in
Physical, psychological, and energy are always consciousnesses
Voluntary addition can be used to make normal parallels equal
The consciousness of this Samadhi is the voice of the basic elements |1|

Yatha Atharva

It is false that this Atharva Veda is the Rakshasa Veda
Like the other three Vedas, it is also an Apaurusheya
It is the measurement itself that tells us the strategy
Thus, we should be grateful for great Rishi's analogy |1|

These Atharva mantras are the juice of the organs
These juices are medicinal forms of fortunes
These medicines are the ambrosia forms
These ambrosia forms are Brahma's norms |2|

Along with blood, flesh, marrow, bone, fat,
sap, and semen are the other basic elements

A description of the organ juices is in the treatment
It is called Bhishagveda in order, according to the therapist |3|

In the Atharva Veda, only nine types of branches are obtainable
Only the Pippalada and Shaunaki samhitas are now available
These samhites, which prescribe intellect, are necessary for life
The implementation is useless if it doesn't come into one's life |4|

He alone is that omnipotent and omnipresent God
He himself has conceived all these divine qualities
Creation, condition, and destruction are born of that Lord
This argument about many gods is an illusion in this world |5|

This Atharva Veda has remedies for problematic fates
It talks about how one can take his mind into a subtle state
The Atharva Veda explains the science of hypnosis
It gives solutions for urination problems for humans |6|

The Atharva Veda says that water contains medicine
It also claims that there is heart disease prevention
The Atharva Veda also describes electrical therapy in detail
It says to speak softly so as not to get the disease's mock-tail |7|

The birth of genius

Atharva says seven elements are responsible for this creation
There are three principles to the state of creative propagation
Human beings have to know the 21 sources of creative action
Intellect means knowing these things through the Vedic convocation |1|

True and pure knowledge should not turn its back on man
The knowledge gained should never be wasted by humans
This knowledge manifests itself in the form of deeds
It can be earned and used at the mercy of witness feeds |2|

Alleviation of disease

When God and nature are thought of as mother and father
When one has left the feeling of hatred and utter fear
That radiance alleviates the effects of many kinds of diseases
A sacred thread with the Brhama festival protects and eases |1|

Intra-human trading will be smooth in the spirit of alliance
This health is well suited to natural remedies with brilliance

Rain, wind, water, moon, and this sun are the real adjectives
One needs to carefully observe these forms of subjectiveness |2|

This water is an elixir in Indian philosophy
Medicine, in this sense, is a scientific topography
This divine water is rich in disease relief
Electrical energy lies in the flow of water, is a belief |3|

Purification of the body is possible with pure water
The inner mind will be purified by the pure body
Purification of austerity is possible in purity of mind
This environmental purity is the aspiration of the Vedic kind |4|

Advice

God Agni is called Lord, King, and Brahmavida
The sacrificers manage the world with Agni Deva
Indra and Agni are interpreted as Paraman and Jivatman
The perverts will be defeated by the brilliance of these Devans |1|

In the Vedas, Ishvara is called instrumental causes
Denomination of life are called ordinary causes
This Mother Nature is called the supportive cause
So, the Vedas should be celebrated without pause |2|

All local beings will benefit from that great Mahat's grace
They will get wealth, mind, charity, knowledge, and brilliance
The local Sadhaka in achievement will find bliss' advice
Elevation is attainable for those who make sacrifices |3|

These Yamas, along with Niyamas, are fierce with the truth
Untruth, violence, and unrighteousness are utter Ruth
These local living beings really cannot resist divine wrath
Thus, we have to know the minds of those who had divine baths |4|

Symptoms of headache, cough, and pain appear in organs
These can be overcome through Adana and Pradanas
Thus, plants need to be propagated in the mountainous regions
Look, disease is born from water, soil, air, and heat pollution |5|

This electric brilliance is nothing but divine lightness
This dispels darkness everywhere with its brightness
There must be a sense of its light in the inner being
Through austerity, it should be enlightened with meaning |6|

There should be prosperity from a female, like a flower
All housewives should live with dignity, using their power
Her husband should protect her soul with his charisma
The Veda is the essence of protection in this charisma |7|

A Yagnya performed on the banks of flowing rivers,
in a forest filled with the spirit of air brilliance,
is dear to that omniscient and omnipotent Isha Lord
All sacrifices should be made for the sake of the world |8|

This Agni is the general who kills the ugly and wicked
He is the slayer of robbers, witches, and the crooked
Local real priests wrestle with the use of white lead
This is the way to win the war by using Agni's brigade |9|

These penancers remove the handicaps of life's demands
The fortune is intimated by the gods at their commands
Bad character, symptoms, and practices should be pushed
By Mantra's preaching, inauspiciousness has to be cleansed |10|

The virtue of sacrifice removes every kind of evil
of hidden enemies as well as hostile enemies,
manifest enemies who wish ill luck local lives
This brilliance is the shield that protects the sadhus |11|

Protection lies under the shelter of that great Lord Varuna
Defeats and sorrows cannot touch the practitioner of Varuna
Because of Deva Varuna, evil tricks will never be able to hurt the beings
Thus, the Vedic assurance has to be looked upon by earthly beings |12|

Our great, omniscient Lord Aditya cures any heart ailments
Even jaundice is removed by Aditya with his red filaments
Aditya's golden rays give beauty and vitality to human lives
He keeps the disease control in the plant with green leaves |13|

This plant medicine on earth will normally be born at night
It treats leprosy and white patches by giving them a tough fight
Herbal medicine removes skin diseases if it is properly implemented
Thus, this medical key, which is Vedic science, should not be neglected |14|

In the shadow of the heroic man lies the achievement for the practitioners
This masculinity is the protection for the essences in the missioners
Thus, these sages are asking Kshatra Tejas of human beings
The meaning of Kshetra Tejas lies in devotion to divine strings |15|

This spirit, which is in the winning, imparts inspiration
This infuses strength into the body through calibration
Only through invincibility does the empress accept humans
The total meaning of this is present in the Vedas vibrations |16|

It is this power of Atman that is the bulwark of life forever
It is the power that actually destroys enemies' interiors
True self-reliance will be the salvation of the nation
Wellness is born in society through self-determination |17|

People must always protect their king as well as the nation
These ascetics should make people aware through good notation
Enemies within are more dangerous to the country than anyone
These calamities born of perversion are psychoses of humans |18|

Nishkamas, Sakamas, Haviya Grahanas, Satvikas,
and Sadhakas have to be observed by the king
They should be counted as true and pure elites in his kingdom
The king has to bear the burden of protecting these five systems |19|

These primal essences and these natural principles are to be
honoured by the sacrifice made in the dedication of the oblations
This is because they are located in each and every direction
It is a dedication to the World President through oblation |20|

One has to know the original Pakriti through the will of the universe
It should be understood that this takes refuge in a Brahman's observance
Life has to greet the symbols of the existence of the Supreme Lord
Brahman's awareness and know-how are to be congratulated on board |21|

Truth and falsity are determined on the basis of walk and talk
Wearing brilliance brings prosperity to the world without break
The inner being is purified by the touch of a gentleman's consensus
By them, one can know that awareness is in pure consciousness |22|

There should be divine sweetness in attitude and interest
This sweetness should shine through in speech and in sight
Sportsmanship is evident in the passion for consuming such sweetness
But this sweetness cannot be born unless one desires self-righteousness |23|

Sinners will never be able to obstruct the glory of a good person
So that the celibacy should be practiced first through retention
Life will be prolonged by the retention of the great Lord Brahman
Along with water and fire, the essence of nature also resides in Paraman |24|

The principle that is the origin of the universe is in the cave of the heart
Based on this, Mother Nature creates the world along with a divine plot
So that every Yogi will always realise this great Brahman principle
Therefore, every Yogi will be called great in the world of acceptable |25|

Life first circumnavigates the emotional world
Later, he will also start to orbit the entire world
When everything is over, he initiates the Brahman principle
It is his inquiry that is the reason for life to be this flexible |26|

Gandharva is the voice of Mother Earth and Lord Sun
Apsara means a life force that moves freely in water
Apsaras are said to be the wives of Gandharva in an application
It is implied in relation to the life force of God's mobilisation |27|

All the pure powers of the world are eternally divine's grace
Coming out of impositions is the breakthrough to life force
These Jyotis are Samhita, which remove ignorance
Thus, one has to understand the mantras' importance |28|

Local life can progress only if it relinquishes the sin,
taming pollution as well as subduing error
A seeker who strives for development should know this
Personality will be formed only by the soul's brilliance |29|

Along with the seven pranas, the eight glands
have to be penetrated by Brahman knowledge
This committed life then becomes an angel of God
Then, in bliss, he can also take shelter in that Lord |30|

That omnipotent Lord has given us a body worthy of wearing
He has commanded from the innermost being to develop everything
Awareness of self-righteousness is hidden in coexistence
This is the secret formula for longevity in this existence |31|

This nature is fearless because it obeys the world order
The past and future are also moving without fear
In God's mercy, there is no fear for local birth
His mercy is to be seen, because fear is death |32|

Along with Ojas, these powers of patience, Darshan, and Ayus,
as well as protective brilliance, are essential for development
The practitioner should be eager for the proper attainment of these
It is a concentrated devotion to lead in the achievement of deeds |33|

Overcoming antagonism with brilliance, progress can be seen
A good career can win the enemy's mind as a true dean
One can act in life with the light of heart and mind
Violence can be alleviated through non-violence's mind |34|

These ascetics look at life with conscious pendency
These pioneers truly have a brilliant-type tendency
Those who have this restraint see life in everything
These wise rise from the limbs and see bliss' bing |35|

These knowledge and deed perceptions are for the Yagnic combination
It is an offering of desire through hearing, remembrance, and meditation
It is a pure vision of truth, as seen in severe penance
This oblation in sacrifice is universal karma with grace |36|

One who is capable must drive away the evil forces within him
He has to subdue hostility with the great essence's limb
Six of these enemies have to surrender in the innermost
These should be hypnotised on the fire and water coasts |37|

The jivatman must declare his dominion over the soul
He should worship this body in the Gayatri and Brihati bowls
Six enemies must be vanquished with tremendous strength
In the end, a state should be established for divine wavelength |38|

This body is acquired for life in the form of its past memories
In self-religion, there is karma, which should rule the mind's calories
The goal of reaching the Supreme is already within you with bliss
The work has provided the senses of knowledge and karma for this |40|

Along with the field, great brilliance has also been given to minds
After making the statute, put the weapons in your hands
Nature has poured Soma into you for the sake of consciousness
We have to allow ourselves to be selfless in seeing the cause of pureness |41|

This water is called a river because of the sound it makes while flowing
This is called Aapaha because it is close to where everyone is when rowing
This water is called Udaka because it travels on earth
Thus, this Vedic literature is the greatest song of its birth |42|

This world is in good condition due to the air and sun
Thus, these sadhakas praise them more than anyone
This love for each other is born out of divine nature
Hence, the will to donate is produced in their feature |43|

The sacrificial Agni is eternally within everything for good
This Agni is the seat of pleasure as well as body and food
Along with the worry, the Agni of hostility also needs to be calmed
This Agni, which is within the universe, is eternally within you |44|

In the eastern direction are the ascetics to protect from destruction's arranger
In the southern direction, there are Purushas who protect those in danger
There are Divya Purushas who have talents in the western direction
All living beings are protected by these people with utter affection |45|

In the north, there are heroes who penetrate the distortions
Divine doctors are protecting us from the polar directions
In the upper direction, there are defence thumbs
We have to get experimental knowledge from them |46|

God Agni is the lord of the eastern direction
Indra dev is situated in the southern direction
They protect the gentlemen with shining weapons
and punishes God-haters in many ways in seconds |47|

Varuna is the lord of the western direction
Soma is shining in the northern direction
By the grace of Varuna, this food, etc., is to be obtained
Lord Soma uses the knowledge as a weapon that is gained |48|

The lower direction is an equally pervasive form of God
The upward direction is the energy form of the Lord
This greenery is great God's weapons' true keys
This form of his power is to protect the devotees |49|

This Lord's power is the prime mover of creation
Awareness of the un-manifest is true manifest action
Omniscient God inspires the creation of subtle existence
Later, he creates this world out of diversity and persistence |50|

Actually, that great majesty is situated in the awakened state.
He is distinguished by the subtlety of the dream's fates
He is latently moving as a seed in a state of deep sleep's state
God himself is the platform in these three conscious's fates |51|

Along with creation, there is a will for states and destruction
It is always intuitive in its causative and motivating functions
Its play is present in both the birth and death of local humans
All this also means the pure consciousness of that Brahman |52|

In whose glory these worlds are spread,
in whose cause this god Sun shines,
He is the that Brahman and the witness in all
To whom will you surrender other than him? |53|

Beyond this space is the precious world named Dyu
The Atman world is there for the sake of evolution, of due
There is Jyotirloka with material, feelings, and knowledge
This love needs to move upward like this without bondage |54|

The essence of the five fundamentals has to be gained through the senses
This life has to experience sensations through the energy of perceptions
Its essence, which is in all directions, should be realised by life selflessly
The phenomenon of its energy sector attraction is to be seen fearlessly |55|

Supreme and local movements and thoughts exist in this world
If that supreme is infinite, then this local life is just atomized
If local movement and thought roam just in local lives,
that supreme movement and thought reign in the cosmos |56|

Rain brings immense joy to the local living beings
This heart of feeling is thrilled with joy in humans
Dedication is the rain and is an equal gain to God's mercy
Hymns are aporousheya poetry due to the moisture of the feel |57|

The brilliance of this spirit is to show the way with illumination
For the life that is at night, this will show the way with notation
It is in the inauspicious loss that the good will manifest
This creation will take shape in the process of manifestation |58|

Through the fire of penance, the Rishi group gains strength properly
The magic of the Asura group will be stopped by Agni sincerely
That supreme Lord protects us from demonic forces
Thus, the brilliance of Agni has to be realised through focus |59|

The temperance of sages should not be seen as bad
The sacrifices of Sadhus should not be brushed aside
In the sacrifice, they poured the juice with expressiveness
So, blood should not be spent in the stream of selfishness |60|

Physical and spiritual are symbols of mother and father
Both of them give good fortune and good intellect a feather
These will infinitely proliferate in true plan form
Hence, one should become a poet by realising these norms |61|

It is to feel that the essence of the world is Bhava in the act of creation
It is to feel that this is Sharva within the dance of world destruction
These local creatures cannot run away from creation and destruction
Bhava and Sharvas are the ones who can give liberation from the shackles |62|

The words in the Vedic mantras are not just written nouns
Rather, these are the meditations of accomplished beings
These are applied meanings beyond the three natures
In truth, this is the greatest of living and non-living things |63|

The head part is always similar to the Rathantara Sama
The lower part of that great lord is like a Bruhat sama
The stomach is Vamvedya Sama, while Chandus is on both sides
It is from this division that life attains those divine slides |64|

The universe is the seat, and the head itself is Brahman
The stomach is both moving and non-moving, and life is lateral
According to the Vedas, truth is the voice of the world
This realisation of the Mahat principle is Upasana's world |65|

From what one has knowledge of Brahman, from what one has siddhi,
from what one has immortality, from what one has no fear,
from that one has to overcome the fear of death
These are what the Vedic scriptures say |66|

The wealth of the world should be earned through sportsmanship
Goodness in sacrifice should be covered with firm wisdom
So Upasanam should be done with a sense of sacrifice's bliss.
Both physical and mental strength should be acquired like this |67|

Along with shama, dama, titiksha, uprati, the shraddha,
and samadhana are ever the wealth of life
These are the true living forces behind sportsmanship
It is the evolution of life in the cessation of sin's ship |68|

Local life will be blissful only with the divine endowment's glue
One can see the same opinion of the wise in their emotional clue
This sportsmanship can be seen with the inner eye
This cosmic order is present in all space and time's sigh |69|

Along with eyes, mind, knowledge, and austerities
are the real weapons of man, according to Vedic order
Control within these is the real tool of local cleverness
In this way, we can defeat enemies forever with a buzz |70|

We should bow down to the Brilliance, Earth, and Space editions
Our lives should honour the knowledge that lies within our intuitions
There should be a sense of sportsmanship in broad mentality
Then one can find local continuity in external spirituality |71|

This fire, which is lit by Yaga, is meant to spread the divine principle
It brings together those in evolution through time with true vincible
The fire of the sacrifice has to be kindled by the lust of the mind
Then one can really find a place among pure scholars' kind |72|

This physical ability is needed to survive in earthly measures
The voice of this knowledge is needed along with pleasures
These three should also be present in equal proportion
Then this life will be blessed through eternal devotion |73|

For achievement, one must have strength in the eleven senses
There should be firmness in spiritual study, along with houses
Nothing can be achieved in this world with helplessness
There must be a flow of essence in creating newness |74|

All powers take shelter in the wearer of pure consciousness
Aditya and these forces of water always act as he wants
Because of this, he can penetrate unhindered with creativity
Life has to exercise this power with sportsmanship variety |75|

Jealousy of the mind should be removed first
Moods like envy should be eradicated next
These are all the first important steps towards creativity
An emotionless corpse has no elevation in sensitivity |76|

This awareness is realized by worshiping Vaishvanara
In the worship of Taijasa, this latent energy will be awakened
This subtlety is awakened by the worship of Prajnya
Later, the role of a platform for creativity will be realised |77|

Along with energy, moods, mind, intellect,
knowledge, vision, and talent, these visionary energies
are the real means of life in eight ways
The role of these in basic creative business is to be understood |78|

Life force, etc., should be in good condition for achievement
The practitioner has to protect them with the power of speech
These powers of speech are complementary, as in Vedic expression
This Vedic science has to be understood for creative interaction |79|

This nature is atomic, from brilliance to grossness
This is the subtlety in the metamorphosis farces
These gross and subtle parts are the superior and inferior parts
The disturbance of these means good and bad creative arts |80|

This eternal Vedic vox has to be published in immense, deep sounds
The essence of sportsmanship should be worshipped beyond words' bounds
Because of this, when it crosses the conscious, it becomes latent and subtle
The fundamental creativity will then be sensed in the awareness without
battle|81|

Life must realize the secret of his birth and become generous
It should move through the world with philosophical decorousness
Life should think about reality every day without strife
Then the mind with dynamic balance is born into life |82|

This local life has to worship the Supreme in good deeds
Sportsmanship, consistency, and charity are to be sacrificed
This path is like having already achieved the ultimate source of creativity
Because of this, one should respect the Vedic language's perceptibility |83|

The Supreme knows all that is outside as well as all that is inside
Within omniscience, it can manifest creativity throughout life
The powers of Vaishvanara, Taijasa, and Prajna are nurtured by the parent
Awaken, Sushupti, and dreaming are nurtured by the Supreme Content |84|

This Saraswati is a flash that is like moving lightning
She is the divine voice and the flowing stream of water
She is knowledgeable, and she has always been sentimental
Her refuge is sound, and she is creative in fundamental |85|

This Vani within the Vedas is a work of wisdom
This creation by Brahma is Shruti in terms of science
Yagnya has been performed for the sake of the world by Saadhyas
This fundamental creativity within one's life is Vedic in origin |86|

Momentum is the life soul, and vastness is the supreme soul
These elements are significant in the local body cavity
These two principles are actually involved in creativity
Knowing sacrifices in life can help with creative sensitivity |87|

There is a pure vision of knowledge in sportsmanship
In the sense of physicality, this can be called a natural force

This is the reason for the evolution of the potential of paranormals
Man can also do creation with the power of his mind's faculties |88|

The sacrificial fire is combustible, which purifies the environment
These sacrificial substances destroy pathogens without punishment
Because of this, this life needs to do Yagnyam with certainty
This will certainly increase one's life by removing the deformity |89|

This penance is of supreme priority in Vedic attendance
There is intense heat in the awareness of interdependence
It communicates transcendental, infinite bliss
It is an eternal longing to know the truth of the ultimate |90|

The sun and these moons come together on the same date
It is Amavasya, and females join in this same fate
Femininity in masculinity is necessary for the sacrifice of life
This combination is about sparking fundamental creativity in life |91|

Platforms, space, and electricity are products of pure consciousness
The fourth is feeling for life through Vedic consciousness
It is worth knowing this essence, which is within a cause
We have to use these four for creativity without pause |92|

Based on the five natural tanmatras, the vast world counts
This world is built on the five fundamental elements
Our mother, Prakriti, is born from the subtle to the gross
Beyond subtle nature lies the presence of pure consciousness |93|

This electrical energy is the standard measurement of pure consciousness
This pure consciousness is the evidence that transcends the five physical
This creativity will come from the source of pure consciousness
If inner evidence allows, then creativity will happen with fundamentalness |94|

Our inner five senses deal with five functional things
For all five seasons, life is regular in all directions
These are active towards pure consciousness in the actual sense
Thus, creativity is possible if these are allowed to commence |95|

The seven Yagnyas, samidhas, madhus, rutas,
along with ghritas are meant for one's success
These seven Chandus are forever attached to life's mixtures
Within interdependence, these are placed for inner evidence |96|

Vedic Chandus are a method of arrangement in physicality
It is a device that consists of words, letters, and Matra's vitality
These are true sporting forces in emotional environments
They are the way to reach ultimate creativity with endorsements |97|

There are seven sages who are moderators of the seven elements
These living beings are endowed with seven pure qualities
They nourish the five types of living beings in juice varieties
Thus, there is constant creativity in the seven elements and qualities |98|

For ultimate creativity, there are communication styles
Along with para, pasyanti, and madhyamya, there are vaikharis
These voices express the knowledge of that pure consciousness
Para is a medium that turns the spirit into music for creative consensus |99|

This earthly life should consume juice like ambrosia
It should be remembered that knowledge is everywhere
This Ambrosia juice means potential within sportsmanship
Moving attention is fundamental to creativity in relationship |100|

To know the source of knowledge, one should take an interest
He should try to know every organ of this channel with trust
There is a clue to the origin of this channel in Vedic science
When realised, creativity can flow from colour to compliance |101|

This world is expressed in the beauty of truth
This divine essence is the source of activity
This creativity is possible because of the essence of fate
No creativity survives at the evil determination's gate |102|

Sin is tamas, and laziness is inertia
So this life has to do karma in Samsara
The spirit has to be invigorated by the virtues in the elixir
Such awareness is the true source of creative life's spritzer |103|

Along with Aishah, there are natural, Sanchita,
accumulated, Prarabdha, and Agami Karmas for life
All these karmas are also the living memories of the living things
In the purity of these is the end of disorder in human beings |104|

The organs of the pure are the sacrificial materials
If his bones are Ruchas, his hairs are Saamas
If the heart is Yaju, then the outer covering is Hawi
Thus, everything should be purified and dedicated to creativity |105|

All five limbs of Samagana are the gift for creativity
Savita, Usha, Tvashta, and Vaishvanara, including Brihaspati,
are the benefactors of the seeker's activity
These pleasures are the senses in fundamental creativity |106|

In creativity, life must move from the physical to the metaphysical
Then, one should move from the earthly to the spiritual
Then, one must proceed from feeling to database and finally to realization
This pure consciousness is the catalyst for human creative actualization |107|

The creativity to be known by the Gayatri Mantram
It is to find the power of creativity in Upasanam
Creativity is obtained through the recitation of Vedic Vox
Seven types of creativity can be achieved through Chandus' wax |108|

Creativity should be understood with Vedic knowledge
Vedic knowledge should be learned through the senses
Abundant food should be given along with the rain
Only in this way will this creativity take place without pain |109|

This earth is a sacrificial platform for human beings
This sun is the power of discernment for him
Sacrifice is the seat of production for all creativity
Vedic vox is the root cause of everything without mortality |110|

This subtle creativity is within the seven principles
These principles are always based on different qualities
These bases are united by the mind and pure intellect
These permeate life and become means of achievement |111|

Ruche's stanza is within the volume of the time calculation
This actual meaning produces the divine vibration
This pure consciousness is embodied in three feet in this world
Thus, creativity is alive even in the four directions with divine hold |112|

The soul and these bodies are in intimate shelter
These have fostered a relationship with opposite qualities
Life has a progression by using its own form of energy
Because of this, creativity can be spurred on in life |113|

The voice within the Vedas will respond to the cosmos
With the Omkara, it crosses countless feet with nine darshans
It is the energy of the essence of the world in creation
It is because of this that knowledge originates in humans |114|

The first creation was an expression beyond time and space
Later, this principle embraced creativity in both time and space
This creative force is constantly engaged in rules-put forth
It is to act in the manifest world for the preservation of truth |115|

There is a mention of 'Chatwari Padani' in Vedic vox
Spiritualists refer to this as Om, along with Bhuh, Bhuvah, and Swaha
Yajniks call it mantra, kalpa, brahman, and worldly language
Historians call this a serpent, bird, insect, or human's language |116|

Who first gave juices in formations?
Who gave life to the souls of local creations?
The principle of creativity is to be understood
It is the source from which creatures can create |117|

Along with Ruta, truth, effort, Tapass, Diksha, and Brahma,
these sacrifices are the true platforms
These are the mother forms that nurture creativity's bell
These eternals are present for our lives in the future as well |118|

In addition to the fundamental, there is conditional and situational creativity
A person who knows what to do should know about communicative activity
If there is no such thing as trend, this science becomes useless for one
This creativity is not driven by logic within information alone |119|

From Agni, there is birth, and finally, from him, there is cremation
There is a true spirit in one born to the Vedas for creation
Garhapatya, Ahavaneya, and these Dakshina Agnis are there for creativity
These concepts, like those in the physical, are there for the creative
activity|120|

This path of creativity has always been embedded in mystery
Since this is not clear, one has to proceed with inertia itself
This path of creation sees all life as an equal mould
In the ululant, it never comes in handy for anyone in the world |121|

This tendency towards creativity is inherent in life's norm
Even though it appears in diversity, it is in the same form
But local life has to be cultivated for its use
With effort, it will yield true fruit with muse |122|

This universe is eternally full of supreme creative norms
Originating from the Jyoti world, this creativity is in expansive form

These localised structures are always separate from the Jyoti itself
But the wise one can obtain creative brilliance by sacrificing oneself |123|

The rays of the sun are strengthened by the secretion of consciousness
Our holy mother earth is expanded by these Soma juices
This soma is stabilised due to the stars in the cosmos
One needs to know its importance in his creative acts |124|

The two months of spring are guardians of creativity
Brihat and Rathantara Chandus are attendants to this activity
These protect the local sacrificer before his creative acts
The two months of summer are used with Sama's facts |125|

Vairup and Vairaja Chhanda are similar in the Varsha
This will protect the local creative aspirant later
These will give answers for one who has vowed creativity
Shaitya and Naudhasa move together in Sama's activity |126|

Earth and Agni are planned for service in the Hemanta season
A man who takes an oath of creativity in firmness will be protected
Dyu-Loka and Aditya provide services for his creative activities
Thus, the scholar will instantly pulsate with inner sensitivity |127|

When a person decides to create, the air element supports him first
It bestows strength on the one who observes the oath next
One who knows this will wear the garland from the water
This cosmos is the main factor in the creativity of the oath-taker |128|

Pournmasi is the first Apana for a real oath-taker
The second apana is Ashtaka, for creative caretaker
The third Apana is the new moon for the oath-taker
Apana, in the fourth, is diligence for the creative maker |129|

The fifth apanava is initiation for one who is in devotion
Apana in the sixth is a sacrifice to someone who is in motion
Dakshina is the seventh apana for one who is in devotion
Within Apana Pada is the drive for creativity in motion |130|

The first Vyana for the practitioner is Mother Earth
The second Vyana is space for his inner wealth
The third Vyana is the sky for the true devotee
The fourth Vyana is stars for one who has creativity |131|

The fifth Vyana is the season for true devotion
The sixth Vyana is matter in relation to season
The seventh Vyana is Samvatsara for the devotee
Divinity in Vyana is self-actualization in creativity |132|

Creativity should be offered to all living beings in their culture
Yagnya has to be strengthened for the balance of nature
Then this wealth will flow in flood mode in one's life's motion
One needs to know how God sees proportion in Yagnic creation |133|

Creationism has always been paramount to creativity
This creativity has the qualities of a conditioning activity
Local life has to adopt a rhythm of fundamental creativity
Liberation should be the goal of one's creative activity |134|

Creativity can be experienced by the visionary
Basic creativity was actually expanded like the sky
It is to be in the intellect by its own power
In reality, it is to stand for every life forever |135|

There is a wealth of creativity in the principle of Mahat
It forms consciousness with its immense power
Its specialty can be seen in the essence of justice
Vedic science shows the way to creative sequence |136|

Professions of the will have the determination of creativity
Professions are matured by this Sattvik activity
Principles help in taming Rajas and Tama qualities
Later, professions will facilitate life as a form of facility |137|

Yajur

Actions are described by the Yajur-veda in the sense of beneficence
As for action, it suggests the means as well as the organs
If there is firm knowledge in the matter of action, there is happiness
When the cause of the action is realised, it is the actual mindfulness |1|

One who does creation should implement karma in science
Substances, etc., should be used with proper means
He should move around the world with auspicious business
This Yajurveda is meant to explain Karma with liveliness |2|

One should strive for food, juice, and scientific prowess
Dignified creativity should be resorted to with pleasures

The supreme evidence that gives all is to be commended
Creativity should be borne in the cause of world welfare |3|

Creativity has different meanings in the domain of sacrifice
Courtesy of creativity should be treated with essence
Basic creativity requires a demonstration of sculpture
Admiring virtue is the fuel needed for creative culture |4|

In celebrating creativity, this spirit is the achiever
He is the maker of creations in the form of knowledge
There is real happiness in life because of the act of creativity
One has to question voxes and then accept them with sensuality |5|

The first voice of creativity is in Vedic study
Its second voice is in the practice of karmas
The voice that illuminates science is the third in creativity
Creativity can only happen through the practice of self-actuality |6|

Who inspires good karma into self-dharma for creation?
Who shows the true meaning of life within eternal truth?
The answer to these questions lies in the journey of creativity
Vedic science can be understood with this contextual sensitivity |7|

A practitioner has to know the limbs of yoga for creativity
He has to know the principles by using internal activity
The nature of karma should be used with intellect
The work of consciousness has to be used in determination |8|

Knowledge of principles should be acquired through proper food and excursions
Pure consciousness must be realized for creativity through the yogic sciences
The creativity of the practitioner is to bear fruit from the word of truth
Creativity can be enhanced by the practitioner through the feeling of the heart|9|

This Creator should do Homa with perfumes, etc.
Plants should be purified from the air for creativity
Disease should be examined, and then purity should be attained
Then creativity is possible if pure earnings are maintained |10|

One who has creativity should acquire pure knowledge and wisdom
Along with laziness, hypocrites should be abandoned from the system
Through study and teaching, creativity will be well nourished
The creativity of the one who creates in secular society will be flourished |11|

The creator must refine his life with the truth of the cosmic order
A natural electrical form must be held for life forever
Disease and forms of ignorance should be removed
For the sake of creativity, drugs should not be consumed |12|

Vidyas and culinary rites should be learned by the true creator
Saatvic food should be eaten in the best possible manner
Alcohol, meat, laziness, and oversleeping should be avoided
The creation then takes place in accordance with Yama and Niyama's bond 13|

These creative powers transcend both time and space
These are moving in effect within the basic elemental radiance
These energies enter the body through air and green plants
So, these should be identified, taken, and used by inner grants |14|

The creator should ask the scholars of doubt
He has to cultivate love in Ishan's creativity
This science is forever brought to life by testing
Science is to be seen for creativity in self-boosting |15|

Prana should be given a dimension for basic creativity
For dimension, the mind must be controlled by the ability
Mind can be controlled by Prana, and Prana by mind
From the purity, material science of creativity can be gained |16|

There are four ingredients for creation sacrifices
The first one is the nutrient-dense offering material
Purification, Yajnika, and Agni are the next three substances
The sacrifice of creation will be fulfilled by these elements |17|

Electricity is the first effect of a creative act
This principle form of Mahat is the second effect
This nature is the root cause of all creation
Mahat is awareness in the rhythm of creation |18|

The six types of seasons are the pillars of creation
Water, etc.—these things are the business of creation
Local life and non-life are the factors of creation
Knowledge of creation is within these foundations |19|

Rigveda
This entire world is a sacrificial school for creativity
Plants, trees, and the air are examples of selflessness

From one seed, many seeds are born without a ceiling
Creativity takes place in the Vedic style of eternal feeling |1|

There is creativity in wisdom, but there is nothing in repetition
There is science in good karma, but nothing in imitation
Within knowledge-laden karma lies the essence of creativity
Creativity moves within the worship of good quality |2|

One who is pure can find the original flame of creativity
Its beauty can be tasted in non-violence and devotional activity
In five pranas, there is a momentum for creation in this world
Creative spirit can be gained from medicines and herbs' mould |3|

These sages worshipped creation with dedication and devotion
It is realized by those who create from the vox of the Vedas
The yagnya of non-violence is the only way to creativity
This birth can attain an evolution within creative activity |4|

A practitioner should choose from the four forms of speech
For this speech, he needs to know the wind's approach
This speech is the source of knowledge within creativity
If one abandons selfishness, this is available to his sensitivity |5|

By worshipping Agni, the intellect of the creator will be enhanced
When the inner nadis are opened, his life becomes conscious
Yagnya sharpens the mind of the practitioner with motivation
Sacrifice should be done only with the spirit of Yagnya for creation |6|

That Supreme is a witness to Karma, along with Aditya
This creation is aimed at experiencing creativity
Within the vision of revolution lies the secret of creativity
Creativity can be touched within the supreme poetic activity |7|

Gaining knowledge is the only way to be creative
The Four Vedas are the scientific source of knowledge
This life should know the creation from the sky
If time is limited, creativity is infinite to buy |8|

This basic creativity travels in the form of energy
It can be found within the heart through loving kindness
The substances are already within the world for creation
It communicates from above for our locals' activation |9|

A creator should eat foods that contain pure essence
He should speak the truth and follow the words of the sages
He should listen to the voice of the Vedas, which is for creation
Then he can achieve infinite possibilities through true action |10|

These particles of creativity are mixed in the four Vedas
It conveys omnipresence for the basic creative canvas
Creativity takes place in the inner, subtle organs by the samas
It moves in the principle of creation by Rukk and Yajanas |11|

By which karmas this body is nourished,
the mind rejoices, and strength is obtained?
Those should be done faithfully by the soul
Then creativity will come to life in the divine bowl |12|

The reason for creativity is really mystical to humans
Thus, it is experienced through the subtle organs within
For its understanding, there is no other path than the Vedas
One has to realize the basic creativity through Neti ways |13|

There are three purposes in this supreme creation
Karma should be done along with knowledge secretion
The ultimate preservation of this creation is the third one
In coexistence, basic creativity is what sustains humans |14|

These Vedic mantras describe the origin of creation
For this reason, it bestow dominion over creation
In the sense of manhood, one knows what creativity is
Humans must learn by seeing what creative reality is |15|

There are thousands of clusters for creativity
These ingredients for creativity are innumerable
Creativity lies within every particle of the present moment
To see this, one should have equanimity in his awareness content |16|

This creation is more molecular than microscopic
It is greater than the great principle of the cosmos
For the creator, there is a substance of creativity in the exterior
These will move and create within the human being's interior |17|

Rigveda introduces the quality of basic creativity
The Yajur Veda describes the karma of this activity
The Sama Veda addresses the worship of creativity
The Atharva talks about the energy required for this activity |18|

This source of fundamental creativity is in Apourusheya form
This creativity will be brought to life by the Pourusheya norm
Hence, a local creative person has to leave his logic first
Then nature of it should be savoured in a courtesy's nest |19|

For creativity, there is air along with speech in life
Yoga of articulation can be achieved by Vashatkara
Due to Vashatkara, this Sun bears creative activity
Along with rain, there are many factors for creativity |20|

Agni and Soma are the principles of fundamental creativity
In the framework, these are the arrangements for its activity
Lord Agni will glow in the moisture of Soma's juice
Because of Soma, creativity will sing to life's sauce |21|

Our Lord, the eternal Agni, is hidden within all matter
He is travelling in Swah Loka along with Bhu Bhuvah
He creates basic creativity through action and cause
So, the creator should worship Agni without pause |22|

Kundalini must be awakened in life for basic creativity
One should establish the power of Prana in Sahasrara
Then the realisation of creativity takes place within him
The knowledge of the creativity of worlds will then flow within |23|

One should perform yagnyas and yagas for the creative kind
He should always pour out sweetness with a pure mind
This creativity then moves from the yaga within the compounds
Creativity takes place only through the yoga of merit with bounds |24|

With the physical and mental, there should be energy for creativity
One should move with equanimity, as there is peace in the mind
There should be welfare of karma through speech and voice
In coexistence, then, creativity comes to him as per his choice |25|

Eternal as well as daily causes are on this earth for creativity
Along with the earth, seven worlds are there for this activity
For creativity, wearable materials should be used by one
Thus, the creator has to know all the ideas of the world with fun |26|

This basic creativity includes method and constitution
Creation, state, and rhythm are the modes of its activity
One should know its properties before starting to create
The creator has to give up iniquity before fate starts to act |27|

Creativity will be enhanced by Abhyantara Kumbha
In the outer Kumbha, there is intellect for creativity
The creative force within Udana always increases
Basic creativity does not happen in weakness |28|

The local creator must realise the eternal light
The denominator must be known, along with the attraction thirst
For creativity, one must know the cause of production
These karmas should be performed without fluctuation |29|

The creator must examine the pleasures of creation
These should be demonstrated by academic specialization
Fundamental creativity should be truly understood by sequence
Then the act of creativity will actually happen in frequence |30|

The creator should observe the Karma Kanda order every day
He should move with brightness, auspiciousness, and gentleness
Then this creativity takes place on the path of progress
Only in brilliance does this creativity take place with bliss |31|

This creation is free from both union and separation
Thus, it happens in the world from a non-local inclination
This manifests due to a combination of divine principles
Because creativity pervades the world through potential actuals |32|

One who creates should be constantly conscious for twenty-four years
Shiksha, grammar, Nirukta, Chanda, Kalpa, astrology should be known
Sankhya should be understood for creativity with Mimamsa, Nyaya, and yoga
Then these Vedanta special shastras bring down creativity for him |33|

These substances are permanent in flood form
Divya's consent to these is given by Aditi's norm
One needs to grasp which is worthy of its function
Ishwara, Jiva, and Prakriti are the causes of creation |34|

Along with air, electricity has infinite causes and actions
There is awareness from sense to action from knowledge to reason
Electricity enters along with air from perception knowledge
Basic creativity has access to reason through action's bondage |35|

A creator who wants Brahman must first become a poet
He should know about air as well as electricity from poetry
Otherwise, this local creator cannot find Ishan forever
So he has to implement Niyama and Yama without errors |36|

By worshipping Brahma, one can gain knowledge, householders
can gain experience, Vanaprastha can gain aversion, asceticism
can gain sacrifice, the ten senses can gain worship and Samadhi
Then the creator can know his own mind, intellect, will, and ego |37|

Common sense

Secureness, non-violence, and mate-ship are accompanied by bliss
This is evidenced by the type of consciousness in Lord Brahman
Thus, one has to give up its opposites, and the best should be gained
If combined with good qualities, this breadth can be attained |1|

These local human experiences are of four types.
Some are direct, and the rest are indirect modes.
Intuitions that appear in humans will come from indirect types
Brahman can be obtained through direct and indirect means |2|

This local human experience has five factual norms
These are existence, lustre, appearance, name, and forms
The first three are arising from Brahman's aspect
Name and these forms are the fruit of worldly intellect |3|

From truth, there is action, and from action, there is reality
Along with time, there is action due to chance's causality
These dimensions are born of the three natures of Brahman
But there is an actuality that truth cannot be grasped from reality |4|

There is nothing before the rising of cosmic time
There is no how behind the cosmic cause
There is nothing called the how behind the birth of opportunity
Truth-knowledge-infinity is the foundation along with eternity |5|

Brahmanism is the movement of the mind in the universe
Brahmanism is the thought of the mind within the vastness
This vast mind is the Brahman within the universe
If one expands, he can become a Brahman through self-religiousness |6|

This science of the Vedas is needed for cosmic principles
Psychology need to work for the Brahman principles
Know that this Eternal-Truth-Infinity is not that easy
See that our sages have spent their lives in this busy |7|

Vyahruti Upasanam

Om Bhu Swaha
O Agni, wash my lust
Om Bhuvah Swaha
O Vayu, quench my thirst
Om Suvah Swaha
O sun, embrace my body
Om bhurbhuvah suvah Swaha
O Prajapati, live in my soul
Om Shantihi Shantihi Shantihi
O Deva, wash my delusion |

Rudra Upasanam
Namaka Upasanam

Om Namo Bhagavate, Hrim Rudraya
I truly bow to you now, O Bhadraya
Save me from the arrow of anger
Use them today against my danger
This mind trembling at the sight of Rudra
I totally surrendered to your bow, Bhadra
Om namo bhagavate Hrim sharvaya
Please accept my wish, O Rudraya |1|

Om Namo Bhagavate, Hrim Rudraya
I truly bow to you now, O Bhadraya
Wipe away your anger at me
Knock out the selfishness in me
Make me auspicious, as I am your child
I wish I should not move as an angry wild
Om namo bhagavate Hrim sharvaya
Please appreciate my wish, O Rudraya |2|

Om Namo Bhagavate, Hrim Rudraya
I truly bow to you now, O Bhadraya
Hide your real, ferocious form
Please give us joy without harm
Show your auspicious Shiva form
Shine light and bless us in the norm
Om namo bhagavate Hrim sharvaya
Please be kind and calm, O Rudraya |3|

Om Namo Bhagavate, Hrim Rudraya
I truly bow to you now, O Bhadraya
You are the Lord who resides in Kailasa
You are the light that gives protection
Hold the arrows, which are ready to fly
Calmly, you hold our hand for foreword
Om namo bhagavate Hrim sharvaya
Please you give us light, O Rudraya |4|

Om Namo Bhagavate, Hrim Rudraya
I truly bow to you now, O Bhadraya
By surrendering to the world, I pray to you
I now ask for release from Discord
Get rid of disease, fear, and bitterness now
Give togetherness in amicable coexistence
Om namo bhagavate Hrim sharvaya
Please correct my pace, O Rudraya |5|

Om Namo Bhagavate, Hrim Rudraya
I truly bow to you now, O Bhadraya
Now stand for me, Mahadeva
As a doctor, see my inner voice
You are the foremost of all divine deities
You are valuable in destroying the enemies
Om namo bhagavate Hrim sharvaya
Meet the essence tone, O Rudraya |6|

Om Namo Bhagavate, Hrim Rudraya
I truly bow to you now, O Bhadraya
This sun rises with a coppery red color
He is auspicious and in true Rudra form
Hey, Rudras, you are actually surrounding us
You are holding on to religion with your anger
Om namo bhagavate Hrim sharvaya
Abandon anger and bless me, O Rudraya |7|

Om Namo Bhagavate, Hrim Rudraya
I truly bow to you now, O Bhadraya
You rise within the red glow, O Rudra
You have a black throat, O Bhadra
Living beings look up to you every day
They are asking you to overcome difficulties
Om namo bhagavate Hrim sharvaya
Please be calm and bless me, O Rudraya |8|

Om Namo Bhagavate, Hrim Rudraya
I truly bow to you now, O Bhadraya
He who has a thousand eyes is our Nilakantta
Indra, who is with the gangs, is the leader for us
Loosen your bow string for good people
Keep the arrow away from the sight of wrath
Om namo bhagavate Hrim sharvaya
Please secure our life, O Rudraya |9|

Om Namo Bhagavate, Hrim Rudraya
I truly bow to you now, O Bhadraya
Put down hundreds of quivers now
Now you blunt the edge of the wand
Show the auspicious Shiva form for this life
Endure these lives for the sake of well-being
Om namo bhagavate Hrim sharvaya
Please save these lives, O Rudraya |10|

Om Namo Bhagavate, Hrim Rudraya
I truly bow to you now, O Bhadraya
You are the owner of the braid with the Kapardi bow
Mridaya, who blows off the head with an arrow?
Reduce the sharpness of ferocious arrows
Bring down this power of scabbard for the good
Om namo bhagavate Hrim sharvaya
Protect those who believe, O Rudraya |11|

Om Namo Bhagavate, Hrim Rudraya
I truly bow to you now, O Bhadraya
Surrender to this bow of yours and salute
This mind is waiting for your blessing's flute
May these weapons of yours protect the good
Let the prowess of the shoulder punish the demons
Om namo bhagavate Hrim sharvaya
Know those surrendered ones, O Rudraya |12|

Om Namo Bhagavate, Hrim Rudraya
I truly bow to you now, O Bhadraya
May these arrows of yours protect me in every way
But let these be far from us forever, from every bay
You know the depth of our minds with the third eye
You often open your eyes to destroy the tripura
Om namo bhagavate Hrim sharvaya
Know that I am afraid, O Rudraya |13|

Om Namo Bhagavate, Hrim Rudraya
I truly bow to you now, O Bhadraya
You are the radiance in all fires
You are the light that burns this universe
As Agni of time, you have three eyes
You are Mrutyunjaya and Mahadev
Om namo bhagavate Hrim sharvaya
Look, I'm surrendered, O Rudraya |14|

Om Namo Bhagavate, Hrim Rudraya
I truly bow to you now, O Bhadraya
Salute to the one who endured the pain of poison
Salute to the conqueror of this great death
Salute to the meditator in this world of turmoil
Salute to the One who preserves in the flood
Om namo bhagavate Hrim sharvaya
Make me like you, O Rudraya |15|

Om Namo Bhagavate, Hrim Rudraya
I truly bow to you now, O Bhadraya
My salute to the Lord of the Four Directions
My salute to the one with golden arms
My salute to the giver of green leaves
Salute to you, who are the leader of animals
Om namo bhagavate Hrim sharvaya
I surrender to you, O Rudraya |16|

Om Namo Bhagavate, Hrim Rudraya
I truly bow to you now, O Bhadraya
Salute to the giver of brightness for color
Salute to the one who shows the true path
Salute to the one who is on Taurus and reaches the goal
Salute to the great God who gives bounties of food
Om namo bhagavate Hrim sharvaya
Please understand my deeds, O Rudraya |17|

Om Namo Bhagavate, Hrim Rudraya
I truly bow to you now, O Bhadraya
My salute to the one with dark hair
My salute to him who wears the yajnopaveeta
My salute to the destroyer of worldly life
My salute to the one who saves the world with a bow
Om namo bhagavate Hrim sharvaya
Drive away this sorrow, O Rudraya |18|

Om Namo Bhagavate, Hrim Rudraya
I truly bow to you now, O Bhadraya
My salute to the receiver in the field
My salute to the invincible
My salute to the incomparable charioteer
My salute to the Lord of the Forest
Om namo bhagavate Hrim sharvaya
Show the right way, O Rudraya |19|

Om Namo Bhagavate, Hrim Rudraya
I truly bow to you now, O Bhadraya
My salute to the one who deals with the meeting
My salute to the one with thick locks of hair
My salute to the Lord, who spread creation
My salute to God, who is dear to the faithful
Om namo bhagavate Hrim sharvaya
Urge me to be faithful, O Rudraya |20|

Om Namo Bhagavate, Hrim Rudraya
I truly bow to you now, O Bhadraya
Salute to the one who wipes out the enemy
Salute to the leader of brave warriors
Salute to the one who surrounds enemies
Salute to one who keeps the good from running away
Om namo bhagavate Hrim sharvaya
Drive away my cowardice, O Rudraya |21|

Om Namo Bhagavate, Hrim Rudraya
I truly bow to you now, O Bhadraya
My salute to him who faces the enemy blow
My salute to him who defeats them
Salute to the one who makes war in all directions
Salute to the one who cuts off the enemy's head
Om namo bhagavate Hrim sharvaya
Teach me not to run away from the battle, O Rudraya |22|

Om Namo Bhagavate, Hrim Rudraya
I truly bow to you now, O Bhadraya
My salute to the leader of all wars
My salute to the one who wields the arrow from the bow
My salutations to the one who punishes thieves
My salutations to the one who protects forever
Om namo bhagavate Hrim sharvaya
Bless me not to lose the battle, O Rudraya |23|

Om Namo Bhagavate, Hrim Rudraya
I truly bow to you now, O Bhadraya
Salute to the one who gives the shield of protection
Salute to the one who inspires the killing of enemies
My salute to the preserver of wealth and crops
My salute to him who moves with a sword
Om namo bhagavate Hrim sharvaya
Make me a warrior, O Rudraya |24|

Om Namo Bhagavate, Hrim Rudraya
I truly bow to you now, O Bhadraya
I salute your bow as well as your arrows
Salute to the hand that wields the arrow
My salutations to the bow stringer
My salute to the one who flies the wands
Om namo bhagavate Hrim sharvaya
Protect me from arrows, O Rudraya |25|

Om Namo Bhagavate, Hrim Rudraya
I truly bow to you now, O Bhadraya
My salute to the sitting and sleeping Rudras
My salute to you, who are asleep and awake
My salute to the standing and running Rudras
My salute to you as a member and as president
Om namo bhagavate Hrim sharvaya
Protect me in action, O Rudraya |26|

Om Namo Bhagavate, Hrim Rudraya
I truly bow to you now, O Bhadraya
O Rudra, in the form of a horse, I salute you
O Rudra, seated on a horse, my salute to you
My salute to those who strike from all directions
My salute to Shakta Devi in form and terror in form
Om namo bhagavate Hrim sharvaya
Give me protection, O Rudraya |27|

Om Namo Bhagavate, Hrim Rudraya
I truly bow to you now, O Bhadraya
My salute to those who are at the forefront of greed
My salute to the pioneers of group breeding
My salute to the presidents of the different gangs
My salute to the weird shape guesser
Om namo bhagavate Hrim sharvaya
Wash away my evil, O Rudraya |28|

Om Namo Bhagavate, Hrim Rudraya
I truly bow to you now, O Bhadraya
My salute to the little ones who are with the big ones
Salutations to those in chariots and those on foot
My sincere salute to the lords of the chariots
My sincere salutations to the army chiefs
Om namo bhagavate Hrim sharvaya
Excuse my pettiness, O Rudraya |29|

Om Namo Bhagavate, Hrim Rudraya
I truly bow to you now, O Bhadraya
My sincere regards to those who travel in vehicles
My salute to the carpenters who make the chariot
My salute to the potters who make the pots
\My salute to the blacksmiths who work in metal
Om namo bhagavate Hrim sharvaya
Please shape me, O Rudraya |30|

Om Namo Bhagavate, Hrim Rudraya
I truly bow to you now, O Bhadraya
My salute to those in fruit-flower form
My salute to those in the form of chicken-fish
My salute to those in the form of a bow and arrow
My salute to those who hunt with Bhairava
Om namo bhagavate Hrim sharvaya
Bear all kinds of fruit, O Rudraya |31|

Om Namo Bhagavate, Hrim Rudraya
I truly bow to you now, O Bhadraya
My salute to the One who is the root of everything
My sincere salute to the destroyer of evils
\My salute to the saviors of lives in detention
Salute from my heart to the blue and white throat
Om namo bhagavate Hrim sharvaya
Endure this world, O Rudraya |32|

Om Namo Bhagavate, Hrim Rudraya
I truly bow to you now, O Bhadraya
My salutations to those with braided locks
My salutations to all hair types in the world
My salute to the one who has a thousand eyes
My salute to those who have a hundred bows
Om namo bhagavate Hrim sharvaya
Put me in yoga, O Rudraya |33|

Om Namo Bhagavate, Hrim Rudraya
I truly bow to you now, O Bhadraya
My salute to those who live on the mountain
My salute to those within Vishnu's heart
My salute to those who bless lives
My salute to Vaman's incarnation in dwarf form
Om namo bhagavate Hrim sharvaya
Please join my heart, O Rudraya |34|

Om Namo Bhagavate, Hrim Rudraya
I truly bow to you now, O Bhadraya
My sincere salutations to the sublime divine
My salute to those who possess greatness
My salute to those who are praised by the scriptures
My salute to those who are eternally ancient
Om namo bhagavate Hrim sharvaya
Put decency in me, O Rudraya |35|

Om Namo Bhagavate, Hrim Rudraya
I truly bow to you now, O Bhadraya
My sincere salutations to the ancients
My salutations to the all-pervading one
My sincere salutations to the swift mover
My salute to the one who moves in the waterfall
Om namo bhagavate Hrim sharvaya
Give me the divinity, O Rudraya |36|

Om Namo Bhagavate, Hrim Rudraya
I truly bow to you now, O Bhadraya
My salute to the One who moves in great waves
My salute to the one who moves in still waters
My salute to the one who moves in the flood
My salute to the one who moves on islands
Om namo bhagavate Hrim sharvaya
Move inside me, O Rudraya |37|

Om Namo Bhagavate, Hrim Rudraya
I truly bow to you now, O Bhadraya
My salute to the elder and to the younger
My salute to the firstborn-after-born
My salute to the undeveloped
My salute to the mover in the middle
Om namo bhagavate Hrim sharvaya
Give me a vision, O Rudraya |38|

Om Namo Bhagavate, Hrim Rudraya
I truly bow to you now, O Bhadraya
For one who moves from behind as well as from below
For one who moves in a world mixed with good
For one moves as well as remains immovable
For one moves in Yama along with Niyama
Om namo bhagavate Hrim sharvaya
Please grant me Yama, O Rudraya |39|

Om Namo Bhagavate, Hrim Rudraya
I truly bow to you now, O Bhadraya
For one who is in rich paddy fields
To one who is praised by Vedic mantras
To him who is described in the Vedic mantra
To him who is in the forest, the shade, the tree
Om namo bhagavate Hrim sharvaya
Save Mother Nature, O Rudraya |40|

Om Namo Bhagavate, Hrim Rudraya
I truly bow to you now, O Bhadraya
For one who sounds in return with the voice
For one who moves swiftly with an army
To him who mounts the chariot and travels
For one who penetrates the plot of the enemy
Om namo bhagavate Hrim sharvaya
Hold my hand in battle, O Rudraya |41|

Om Namo Bhagavate, Hrim Rudraya
I truly bow to you now, O Bhadraya
For one who wears armor for self-protection
To one who has provided protection for the charioteer
To whom these Vedic mantras are appreciated
To him who gathers troops and praises the army
Om namo bhagavate Hrim sharvaya
Give me eternal protection, O Rudraya |42|

Om Namo Bhagavate, Hrim Rudraya
I truly bow to you now, O Bhadraya
For one who holds a stick to beat the drums
For one who never backs down in battle
To one who comes and lands for a special purpose
To the messenger who comes with arrows
Om namo bhagavate Hrim sharvaya
Please give bravery, O Rudraya |43|

Om Namo Bhagavate, Hrim Rudraya
I truly bow to you now, O Bhadraya
To one who blows off the head with a wand
To one who travels even on narrow paths
For one who walks on the highway
For one who descends from high to low
Om namo bhagavate Hrim sharvaya
Show me the way, O Rudraya |44|

Om Namo Bhagavate, Hrim Rudraya
I truly bow to you now, O Bhadraya
For one who dwells in marshy lakes
To one who wanders in flowing rivers
For one who plays in mountain waters
For one who has stayed in wells
Om namo bhagavate Hrim sharvaya
Give me the nourishment of water, O Rudraya |45|

Om Namo Bhagavate, Hrim Rudraya
I truly bow to you now, O Bhadraya
For one who moves briskly in a drought
For one who becomes a drop of rain in autumn
To him who travels like lightning in the clouds
For one who descends as light for the sun
Om namo bhagavate Hrim sharvaya
Give Gayatri and Savitri, O Rudraya |46|

Om Namo Bhagavate, Hrim Rudraya
I truly bow to you now, O Bhadraya
To the one who pours rain with hail
For one who resides in houses as wealth
To him who is the husband of goddess Uma
Salutations to the rose-red one
Om namo bhagavate Hrim sharvaya
Sanction the goddess' grace, O Rudraya |47|

Om Namo Bhagavate, Hrim Rudraya
I truly bow to you now, O Bhadraya
To the one who gives comforts to the worldly life
To him who creates fear in the enemies
To the slayer of demons from afar
To him who draws all within himself in the deluge
Om namo bhagavate Hrim sharvaya
Give Savitri's potential, O Rudraya |48|

Om Namo Bhagavate, Hrim Rudraya
I truly bow to you now, O Bhadraya
To one who dwells in the great divine tree
To the one who is the essence of the Pranava Mantra
To the one who gives comfort to this and that world
For one who is inherent in the main principle
Om namo bhagavate Hrim sharvaya
Give Gayatri's potential, O Rudraya |49|

Om Namo Bhagavate, Hrim Rudraya
I truly bow to you now, O Bhadraya
To him who is auspicious in all auspiciousness
To one who is established on both banks
To the one who lifts from the ravages of sins
To one who assists in crossing life with knowledge
Om namo bhagavate Hrim sharvaya
Give auspiciousness to this life, O Rudraya |50|

Om Namo Bhagavate, Hrim Rudraya
I truly bow to you now, O Bhadraya
To one who is reborn again and again in this world
To one who experiences karma in the form of life
To one who moves in the form of grass and foam
To one who cares in the form of sand and water
Om namo bhagavate Hrim sharvaya
Destroy my karmas, O Rudraya |51|

Om Namo Bhagavate, Hrim Rudraya
I truly bow to you now, O Bhadraya
For one who resides in rough terrain with rocks
For one who ties a braid and wears it likes a crown
To the one who stands directly for the devotees
To one who resides with the cows and in the courtyard
Om namo bhagavate Hrim sharvaya
Give me your kind mind, O Rudraya |52|

Om Namo Bhagavate, Hrim Rudraya
I truly bow to you now, O Bhadraya
For one who reclines on couches
To one who rests in the courtyard of the house
To one who dwells in impenetrable forests
For one who enters mountain caves
Om namo bhagavate Hrim sharvaya
Give me courage like you, O Rudraya |53|

Om Namo Bhagavate, Hrim Rudraya
I truly bow to you now, O Bhadraya
For the one who is in dew drops and water
To him who is in the invisible and visible dust
For one who is inside dry and green things
To him who dwells in the grass and in the desert
Om namo bhagavate Hrim sharvaya
Give firmness like you, O Rudraya |54|

Om Namo Bhagavate, Hrim Rudraya
I truly bow to you now, O Bhadraya
To one who flies in the sky from the earth
For one who is in fair waves
For the lord of the striking Rudra Gang
To the giver of sorrow in bits and pieces
Om namo bhagavate Hrim sharvaya
Eliminate this duality, O Rudraya |55|

Om Namo Bhagavate, Hrim Rudraya
I truly bow to you now, O Bhadraya
Giver of wealth to one who resides in God
To Mahadeva, who is never subject to decay
To Lord Rudra, who examines everything
To the destroyer of all great sins
Om namo bhagavate Hrim sharvaya
Please give me strength, O Rudraya |56|

Om Namo Bhagavate, Hrim Rudraya
I truly bow to you now, O Bhadraya
For one who keeps track of sins and virtues
For one who has assumed gross form
To one who is in the physical form of the universe
For one who dwells in the heart of God
Om namo bhagavate Hrim sharvaya
Give spaciousness, O Rudraya |57|

Om Namo Bhagavate, Hrim Rudraya
I truly bow to you now, O Bhadraya
To the one who shows hell in the lives of sinners
For one who distributes food in the spirit of sport
For one who has black on the neck and red elsewhere
To the possessor of all greatest wealth
Om namo bhagavate Hrim sharvaya
Forgive my sin and lead me, O Rudraya |58|

Om Namo Bhagavate, Hrim Rudraya
I truly bow to you now, O Bhadraya
You are the owner of all our great wealth
We are the ones who live in poverty
Don't you ever scare our close friends
Do not destroy us with sickness
Om namo bhagavate Hrim sharvaya
Have mercy on this life, O Rudraya |59|

Om Namo Bhagavate, Hrim Rudraya
I truly bow to you now, O Bhadraya
Your form is auspicious with peace
It is helpful for life on a daily basis
It removes the ignorance in life
It removes the misery of the world
Om namo bhagavate Hrim sharvaya
Give happiness to this life, O Rudraya |60|

Om Namo Bhagavate, Hrim Rudraya
I truly bow to you now, O Bhadraya
If one pours out sweet sentiments about Rudra,
One can realize that he is the destroyer of enemies
If the strength of mind about Rudra is increased,
One can realize that he is the true savior
Om namo bhagavate Hrim sharvaya
Give me the inner eye, O Rudraya |61|

Om Namo Bhagavate, Hrim Rudraya
I truly bow to you now, O Bhadraya
Give happiness here and in that world
Destroy the sins of worshippers
Deliver him from the sorrow, which follows you
Give your favors and be kind
Om namo bhagavate Hrim sharvaya
Grant me freedom, O Rudraya |62|

Om Namo Bhagavate, Hrim Rudraya
I truly bow to you now, O Bhadraya
O Rudra, do not harm the elderly
Hey, Rudra, don't hurt the girls
O Rudra, do not disturb the child, the youth
Hey, Rudra, don't bring disease to our bodies
Om namo bhagavate Hrim sharvaya
Give me a healthy life, O Rudraya |63|

Om Namo Bhagavate, Hrim Rudraya
I truly bow to you now, O Bhadraya
Do not be angry at our transgressions
Do not punish us, even if there is a reason
We will make an offering to you in the fire
We will give you the oblations to calm down
Om namo bhagavate Hrim sharvaya
Grant forgiveness, O Rudraya |64|

Om Namo Bhagavate, Hrim Rudraya
I truly bow to you now, O Bhadraya
Rudra, let this terrible form of yours be far away
Let our children not be disturbed by your anger
Let the enemy warriors not attack us
May your happy form be with us
Om namo bhagavate Hrim sharvaya
Give a helping hand, O Rudraya |65|

Om Namo Bhagavate, Hrim Rudraya
I truly bow to you now, O Bhadraya
You are famous in our hearts
You are terrible, like a raging lion
You are fierce because of the destruction
Protect the one who worships you
Om namo bhagavate Hrim sharvaya
Kill our enemies, O Rudraya |66|

Om Namo Bhagavate, Hrim Rudraya
I truly bow to you now, O Bhadraya
May your weapon give us breadth
May it take away the burden of our sins
God, let your displeasure go away
May your blessings be upon us forever
Om namo bhagavate Hrim sharvaya
Forgive my sins, O Rudraya |67|

Om Namo Bhagavate, Hrim Rudraya
I truly bow to you now, O Bhadraya
Your intentions will never be wrong
Your arrows never miss the target
Please quench the arrows targeting us
Consider these sacrificial deeds of ours
Om namo bhagavate Hrim sharvaya
Protect our children, O Rudraya |68|

Om Namo Bhagavate, Hrim Rudraya
I truly bow to you now, O Bhadraya
Show your most auspicious form
Give good feelings with good thoughts
Get rid of these menacing weapons
Approach us with the Pinaka bow
Om namo bhagavate Hrim sharvaya
Please save us, O Rudraya |69|

Om Namo Bhagavate, Hrim Rudraya
I truly bow to you now, O Bhadraya
Shower the rain of wealth, O great Rudra
Because you are the owner of this, Bhadra
Your weapons should not destroy us
Let them cut off the heads of our enemies
Om namo bhagavate Hrim sharvaya
When will you come to us, O Rudraya |70|

Om Namo Bhagavate, Hrim Rudraya
I truly bow to you now, O Bhadraya
These arms of thine are innumerable
They are armed with numerous weapons
I beg you, O master of these
Abandon the form of anger, please
Om namo bhagavate Hrim sharvaya
I am waiting to see you, O Rudraya |71|

Om Namo Bhagavate, Hrim Rudraya
I truly bow to you now, O Bhadraya
Thou dwell in innumerable forms
You are protecting us in countless ways
I will loosen the strings of your bow
I will turn away the arrows of wrath
Om namo bhagavate Hrim sharvaya
I am waiting for you, O Rudraya |72|

Om Namo Bhagavate, Hrim Rudraya
I truly bow to you now, O Bhadraya
You are moving in the great ocean
Walking between earth and sky
Please loosen the strings of the bows
Carry them far away from sight
Om namo bhagavate Hrim sharvaya
Please give me health, O Rudraya |73|

Om Namo Bhagavate, Hrim Rudraya
I truly bow to you now, O Bhadraya
Kalakuta settled inside the blue throat
The serpent rested in the male Gang
We loosen their bow strings
We keep their bows at a distance
Om namo bhagavate Hrim sharvaya
Protect me from them, O Rudraya |74|

Om Namo Bhagavate, Hrim Rudraya
I truly bow to you now, O Bhadraya
The poison rests in the blue throat
Heaven resides in the white throat
We will loosen the terrible bow strings
We collect the bows at a distance
Om namo bhagavate Hrim sharvaya
Eat the enemy mob, O Rudraya |75|

Om Namo Bhagavate, Hrim Rudraya
I truly bow to you now, O Bhadraya
These grass-colored Rudras are black in color
They are red in color and live in trees
\We will loosen their bow strings
Also, we keep their bows at a distance
Om namo bhagavate Hrim sharvaya
Protect us from enemies, O Rudraya |76|

Om Namo Bhagavate, Hrim Rudraya
I truly bow to you now, O Bhadraya
Hey, Rudras, you will be in food and liquids
And you enter the creatures that eat them
Thus, we loosen your bow strings
And we will keep those bows away
Om namo bhagavate Hrim sharvaya
Protect us from disease, O Rudraya |77|

Om Namo Bhagavate, Hrim Rudraya
I truly bow to you now, O Bhadraya
Hey, Rudras, you feed us and protect us
You Stand alone and defeat our enemies
You will fight with small and big swords
Hey, Rudras, you always protect chastity
Om namo bhagavate Hrim sharvaya
Give all the fortunes, O Rudraya |78|

Om Namo Bhagavate, Hrim Rudraya
I truly bow to you now, O Bhadraya
Hey, Rudra, you are the supreme hero
Hey Bhadra, you come down for us
O Rudra, attack the enemies
O Bhadra, protect pious lives
Om namo bhagavate Hrim sharvaya
I believe you, O Rudraya |79|

Om Namo Bhagavate, Hrim Rudraya
I truly bow to you now, O Bhadraya
For whom are food substances handy
I worship such Rudras with Vedic vox
I will shove the haters in your mouth
I will salute you from all eight directions
Om namo bhagavate Hrim sharvaya
You are my guide in this world, O Rudraya |80|

Om Namo Bhagavate, Hrim Rudraya
I truly bow to you now, O Bhadraya
Who dwells between the earth and the sky
This air is giving you its handle
This rain does the work because of you
I bow down to you from ten directions
Om namo bhagavate Hrim sharvaya
You are my fortune here, O Rudraya |81|

Om Namo Bhagavate, Hrim Rudraya
I truly bow to you now, O Bhadraya
You have a divine fragrance
You are the source of energy
You are the one with three eyes
Oh God, I will worship like this
Om namo bhagavate Hrim sharvaya
Accept me and embrace me, O Rudraya |82|

Om Namo Bhagavate, Hrim Rudraya
I truly bow to you now, O Bhadraya
Deliver me from untimely death
Protect me from unusual deaths
How pumpkins release from plants
like, keep my death easy in the end
Om namo bhagavate Hrim sharvaya
Awaken knowledge within me, O Rudraya |83|

Om Namo Bhagavate, Hrim Rudraya
I truly bow to you now, O Bhadraya
You are on fire; you are moving in water
You are in the plant; you have entered the world
Give immortality and save from death
Wash away ignorance and give enlightenment
Om namo bhagavate Hrim sharvaya
Enough of these births and deaths, O Rudraya |84|

Om Namo Bhagavate, Hrim Rudraya
I truly bow to you now, O Bhadraya
For one with a beautiful and powerful handle
For one who wields a strong bow and arrows
To the proprietor of the storehouses of medicines
Salutations to the publisher of goodwill
Om namo bhagavate Hrim sharvaya
Show your grace, O Rudraya |85|

Om Namo Bhagavate, Hrim Rudraya
I truly bow to you now, O Bhadraya
This hand of mine is strong because of Linga Puja
This mind is oxidized because of Linga Bhajan
Life is breathing through Linga contact
Because of this, my hands have become lucky
Om namo bhagavate Hrim sharvaya
Solve my difficulties, O Rudraya |86|

Om Namo Bhagavate, Hrim Rudraya
I truly bow to you now, O Bhadraya
O Rudra, you are self-death
You have countless death loops
Thus, men will worship you,
And efficiently escaping from nooses
Om namo bhagavate Hrim sharvaya
Save our men, O Rudraya |87|

Om Namo Bhagavate, Hrim Rudraya
I truly bow to you now, O Bhadraya
O destroyer, I worship you
O death, I will offer sacrifice
You are all-pervading and omnipotent
I am asking you to save me from death
Om namo bhagavate Hrim sharvaya
Save me when I'm in trouble, O Rudraya |88|

Om Namo Bhagavate, Hrim Rudraya
I truly bow to you now, O Bhadraya
God, I understood the hymn that invokes you
Manu and Brihaspati reiterated the same
So let the universe be happy
Let the earth not give sorrow to man
Om namo bhagavate Hrim sharvaya
Grant me proper thought, O Rudraya |89|

Om Namo Bhagavate, Hrim Rudraya
I truly bow to you now, O Bhadraya
God, give me sweet fruits
Create the right thoughts in my mind
Fill my words with sweetness
Fill my actions with coexistence
Om namo bhagavate Hrim sharvaya
Give me wisdom, O Rudraya |90|

Om Namo Bhagavate, Hrim Rudraya
I truly bow to you now, O Bhadraya
I speak only sweet words to people
I will do the right thing for the world
O Rudra, please light up my inner being
Train me as the ancestor expects
Om namo bhagavate Hrim sharvaya
Forgive my helplessness, O Rudraya |91|

Chamaka Upasanam

Om Namo Bhagavate, Hrim Rudraya
I truly bow to you now, O Bhadraya
May this god give me food
May he allow me to eat food
May God ensure the purity of the food
May he give me the desire to eat food
Om namo bhagavate Hrim sharvaya
Accept these requests, O Rudraya |1|

Om Namo Bhagavate, Hrim Rudraya
I truly bow to you now, O Bhadraya
Let me be able to chant Vedic mantras
Let me chant them in a certain tone
Let me have mental diligence for hearing
Let me reach the abode of that Lord

Om namo bhagavate Hrim sharvaya
Accept these requests, O Rudraya |2|

Om Namo Bhagavate, Hrim Rudraya
I truly bow to you now, O Bhadraya
May Prana, Vyana, and Udana be in my control
May Samana air with Udana increase in me.
May this knowledge, mind, and word be abundant
May my hearing be sharp along with my sight
Om namo bhagavate Hrim sharvaya
Accept these requests, O Rudraya |3|

Om Namo Bhagavate, Hrim Rudraya
I truly bow to you now, O Bhadraya
Let these senses within me become sensitive
May these fortunes increase along with health
May this body be active till the end
Let this ego be absorbed in you
Om namo bhagavate Hrim sharvaya
Accept these requests, O Rudraya |4|

Om Namo Bhagavate, Hrim Rudraya
I truly bow to you now, O Bhadraya
Let the energies within me shine
May my manhood shine with vigor
May happiness be with me forever
May these organs be exalted
Om namo bhagavate Hrim sharvaya
Accept these requests, O Rudraya |5|

Om Namo Bhagavate, Hrim Rudraya
I truly bow to you now, O Bhadraya
Let my bones and joints be protected
May my life continue with dignity
Let the 36 things be given in righteousness
Let there be a noble thought for the welfare
Om namo bhagavate Hrim sharvaya
Accept these requests, O Rudraya |6|

Om Namo Bhagavate, Hrim Rudraya
I truly bow to you now, O Bhadraya
Let the mind overcome unrighteousness
Let me get the mark of a great personality
Let my inner rages come under control

Let this inner discontent subside
Om namo bhagavate Hrim sharvaya
Accept these requests, O Rudraya |7|

Om Namo Bhagavate, Hrim Rudraya
I truly bow to you now, O Bhadraya
Let external expression be under my control
May this deep mind give eternal sweetness
Let me have control over all kinds of enemies
May I be victorious over iniquity
Om namo bhagavate Hrim sharvaya
Accept these requests, O Rudraya |8|

Om Namo Bhagavate, Hrim Rudraya
I truly bow to you now, O Bhadraya
Let my success be coveted by others
May the charisma within be ever-valuable
Let worldly materials bring me prosperity
May my posterity move with knowledge
Om namo bhagavate Hrim sharvaya
Accept these requests, O Rudraya |9|

Om Namo Bhagavate, Hrim Rudraya
I truly bow to you now, O Bhadraya
May this consciousness be eternally fixed in truth
Let the intellect be bound by Vedic Vox Shastras
Have faith in Vedic science along with discipline
Let prosperity come to me along with money
Om namo bhagavate Hrim sharvaya
Accept these requests, O Rudraya |10|

Om Namo Bhagavate, Hrim Rudraya
I truly bow to you now, O Bhadraya
Let my pride grow towards the city of God
Let these sports games capture my mind
Let these professions of heritage move within me
Let me get good fortune from the rituals of fate
Om namo bhagavate Hrim sharvaya
Accept these requests, O Rudraya |11|

Om Namo Bhagavate, Hrim Rudraya
I truly bow to you now, O Bhadraya
Let me get past and future wealth
Let me get actual entertainment

Let me have a protected path for movement
Let me get the spirituality of this and that world
Om namo bhagavate Hrim sharvaya
Accept these requests, O Rudraya |12|

Om Namo Bhagavate, Hrim Rudraya
I truly bow to you now, O Bhadraya
May the necessities of happiness come to me
Let me have the potential abilities
Let the perfect intellect descend into me
Let me be successful in difficult situations
Om namo bhagavate Hrim sharvaya
Accept these requests, O Rudraya |13|

Om Namo Bhagavate, Hrim Rudraya
I truly bow to you now, O Bhadraya
Let God shower happiness on earth and heaven
Let all merits come to me to attain happiness
Let yogic relationships be found within spirituality
Let my comforts be for the welfare of the world
Om namo bhagavate Hrim sharvaya
Accept these requests, O Rudraya |14|

Om Namo Bhagavate, Hrim Rudraya
I truly bow to you now, O Bhadraya
Let name, fame, and fortune come to me
Let all senior benefactors guide me
Let me get support from the palace parents
Let me get the fortune to protect my wealth
Om namo bhagavate Hrim sharvaya
Accept these requests, O Rudraya |15|

Om Namo Bhagavate, Hrim Rudraya
I truly bow to you now, O Bhadraya
Let the community prosper with adventure and courage
Let the embodiment of Vedic knowledge come to me
Let me have the strength to help the helpless
Let there be obedient service from posterity
Om namo bhagavate Hrim sharvaya
Accept these requests, O Rudraya |16|

Om Namo Bhagavate, Hrim Rudraya
I truly bow to you now, O Bhadraya
Let me gain expertise in agricultural activities

Let this body be free from all diseases
Let me have a long life with strength
Let enemies be far away from me
Om namo bhagavate Hrim sharvaya
Accept these requests, O Rudraya |17|

Om Namo Bhagavate, Hrim Rudraya
I truly bow to you now, O Bhadraya
Let no untimely death touch me
Let no unnatural death come to me
Let me have good sleep without worries
Let every morning come with hope
Om namo bhagavate Hrim sharvaya
Accept these requests, O Rudraya |18|

Om Namo Bhagavate, Hrim Rudraya
I truly bow to you now, O Bhadraya
Let's get a good invitation to good food
May the juice of sweet bounty reach me
Let abundant rain fall for cultivation
Let me get fertile land along with a girl
Om namo bhagavate Hrim sharvaya
Accept these requests, O Rudraya |19|

Om Namo Bhagavate, Hrim Rudraya
I truly bow to you now, O Bhadraya
Let the tree grow to the height of the sky
Let me get gold and these precious stones
Let securities of ownership be available to me
Let the offspring be accompanied by wisdom
Om namo bhagavate Hrim sharvaya
Accept these requests, O Rudraya |20|

Om Namo Bhagavate, Hrim Rudraya
I truly bow to you now, O Bhadraya
By the grace of you, there is a strong body
Pulses are increasing in abundance
Paddy, barley, and ginger are growing
There are wheat, millet, and pulse grains
Om namo bhagavate Hrim sharvaya
Accept these requests, O Rudraya |21|

Om Namo Bhagavate, Hrim Rudraya
I truly bow to you now, O Bhadraya

God, you have given me mountains, and streams
Along with gold, silver, lead, tin, steel, bronze, copper,
forests, land, animals, and birds have been given
You have given these for the benefit of Dharma
Om namo bhagavate Hrim sharvaya
Accept these requests, O Rudraya |22|

Om Namo Bhagavate, Hrim Rudraya
I truly bow to you now, O Bhadraya
God, you have given sacrifices and holy rituals
These are given to those with the potential
In addition, the goal of liberation is given
I know that you have given these to Dharma
Om namo bhagavate Hrim sharvaya
Accept these requests, O Rudraya |23|

Om Namo Bhagavate, Hrim Rudraya
I truly bow to you now, O Bhadraya
You have attached these gods to our senses
You have gathered sacrificial offerings with sense
You created 25 angels to help mankind
You have given us hymns to invite them
Om namo bhagavate Hrim sharvaya
Accept these requests, O Rudraya |24|

Om Namo Bhagavate, Hrim Rudraya
I truly bow to you now, O Bhadraya
Agni and Soma descend from our senses
Shiva and Saraswati respond through our senses
Senses attract both Pusha and Brihaspati
From the senses, Mitra and Varuna come down
Om namo bhagavate Hrim sharvaya
Accept these requests, O Rudraya |25|

Om Namo Bhagavate, Hrim Rudraya
I truly bow to you now, O Bhadraya
Tvashta and Vishnu are available through the senses
Ashwin and Marut depend on sensualities
Vishwa god moves through our inner senses
Now I know that God, Lord Indra, is important
Om namo bhagavate Hrim sharvaya
Accept these requests, O Rudraya |26|

Om Namo Bhagavate, Hrim Rudraya
I truly bow to you now, O Bhadraya
You placed Indra between heaven and earth
You made four directions as His sides
Prajapati is placed on top of Lord Indran
Now I understand the identity of the senses
Om namo bhagavate Hrim sharvaya
Accept these requests, O Rudraya |27|

Om Namo Bhagavate, Hrim Rudraya
I truly bow to you now, O Bhadraya
O Lord, prepare me for the Soma Yagnya
Please send Amsu, Rasmi, Adhabya, Adhipati,
Upanshu, Antharyam, Mitra, Varun, Ashwin,
Pratiprastana, Shukra, Manti, and Vaishvadeva
Om namo bhagavate Hrim sharvaya
Accept these requests, O Rudraya |28|

Om Namo Bhagavate, Hrim Rudraya
I truly bow to you now, O Bhadraya
O Lord, prepare me for the Soma Yagnya
Send Dhruva, Vaishvanara, Ritu Graha,
Ati Graha, Indra, Agni, Veda, Maruta, Indra,
Aditya, Savita, Saraswati, Pusa, and Haryojana
Om namo bhagavate Hrim sharvaya
Accept these requests, O Rudraya |29|

Om Namo Bhagavate, Hrim Rudraya
I truly bow to you now, O Bhadraya
Bless the sacrificial rituals for Yagnya
Send to me samidha, darbha, kunda,
vittha, asana, pot, potra, sadhana,
dravya, pot, fire, havis, and priests
Om namo bhagavate Hrim sharvaya
Accept these requests, O Rudraya |30|

Om Namo Bhagavate, Hrim Rudraya
I truly bow to you now, O Bhadraya
O God, Agni of Yagnya, Pravarga, Arka, Surya,
Prana, Homa, Bhumi, Aditi, Diti, and Swarga,
grant all needs along with the index finger of Yagnyas
Give these for the accomplishments of Yagnya
Om namo bhagavate Hrim sharvaya
Accept these requests, O Rudraya |31|

Om Namo Bhagavate, Hrim Rudraya
I truly bow to you now, O Bhadraya
Give me the Shaktya hymns that are in the Vedas
Show me the Rik, Sama, Adharva, and Yajurvedas
Give me the stoma, diksha, homa, and vratas
Then I will do karma with discipline and diligence
Om namo bhagavate Hrim sharvaya
Accept these requests, O Rudraya |32|

Om Namo Bhagavate, Hrim Rudraya
I truly bow to you now, O Bhadraya
Let the vows and disciplines be consolidated
Let the Bruhati and Rathantara Sama rain down
May the sacrifice of life be successful
Oh great Lord, make my life prosperous
Om namo bhagavate Hrim sharvaya
Accept these requests, O Rudraya |33|

Om Namo Bhagavate, Hrim Rudraya
I truly bow to you now, O Bhadraya
Give protection to cattle, calves, animals, and birds
God, please stimulate all my five senses
Give strength to myself, which means making sacrifices
God, please give me a long life to reach perfection
Om namo bhagavate Hrim sharvaya
Accept these requests, O Rudraya |34|

Om Namo Bhagavate, Hrim Rudraya
I truly bow to you now, O Bhadraya
Oh Lord, you have given us heredity
I know that from 1 to 3, it is odd until 33
You produced food in equal numbers
I know that this action is for our survival
Om namo bhagavate Hrim sharvaya
Accept these requests, O Rudraya |35|

Om Namo Bhagavate, Hrim Rudraya
I truly bow to you now, O Bhadraya
Oh Lord, you are the sun for all kinds of production
You are the earth to teach us what completeness is
This is why you have appointed the god of time
You have permeated everything in administration
Om namo bhagavate Hrim sharvaya
Accept these requests, O Rudraya |36|

Om Namo Bhagavate, Hrim Rudraya
I truly bow to you now, O Bhadraya
I beseech you through Vedic mantras
Manu will worship you through sacrifices
Brihaspati will salute you through a mantra
Have mercy on me, O great Lord
Om namo bhagavate Hrim sharvaya
Accept these requests, O Rudraya |37|

Om Namo Bhagavate, Hrim Rudraya
I truly bow to you now, O Bhadraya
May Vishwa God take away the sorrows in me
May Mother Earth love me happily
May Saraswati make sound in me smoothly
They are waiting for your command, O Lord
Om namo bhagavate Hrim sharvaya
Accept these requests, O Rudraya |38|

Om Namo Bhagavate, Hrim Rudraya
I truly bow to you now, O Bhadraya
Let the worthy words flow from me
Let the people know my happiness
May the ancestors shower me with blessings
Please give wisdom for this, O Lord
Om namo bhagavate Hrim sharvaya
Accept these requests, O Rudraya |39|

Shiksha Upasanam

May Mitra, the patron deity of the day, grant comfort
May Varuna, the patron deity of the night, grant comfort
Because of them, the Apana and Prana move inside
If they curse, no knowledge will ever come inside |1|

May Aryama, the patron deity of the sun, grant comfort
May Indra, the patron deity of strength, grant comfort
Because of them, the eyes and senses move inside
If they curse, no knowledge will ever come inside |2|

May Bruhaspati, the patron deity of the wit, grant comfort
May Urukrama, the patron deity of legs, grant comfort
Because of them, the speech and area move inside
If they curse, no knowledge will ever come inside |3|

A sharpness to hear comes from these patron deities
By worshipping them, knowledge will descend into one to adopt
Awareness is achieved through Swa-Dharma coupled with improved perception
Otherwise, the barrier will move, and the man will fade away into the
creation|4|

Air is given to all without distinguishing between virtuous and sinful
This earthly air provides the fruits of all the karmas of living beings
Thus, the air in the atmosphere is the brahman of this world
It is the smell of karma that disturbs a human's Prana's mould |5|

Pranas nourish the Ruta, which is said to be the world order
This Ruta declares a certain meaning in the intellect
Oh man, know immediately that this is the order of the Vedas
See now that in this world, life itself is nothing but the Rutas |6|

A man should give up lies and tell the truth
This too should be moved by the grace of this Prana
If truth is Brahman, then air should be understood as Brahman here
If we know this, three kinds of difficulties will not trouble us anymore |7|

It is not so easy to gain knowledge from the scriptures
Acquiring knowledge by knowing ignorance is not an easy task
Because these codes are a cluster of colors outward
Only by worshipping these will knowledge move inward |8|

The interpretation of the Upanishads is in these five shelters
These are Adhiloka, Adhijyotisha, Adhividya, Adhipraja, and Adhyatma
Understand that these are known as the Five Great Codes
The features of the study are born out of these nodes |9|

Earth is the past, while Dhyu-loka is the next
If opportunity is meeting, then wind is negotiation
Know that this is the first Adhi-loka for knowledge
If none of these happen, learning cannot happen |10|

Fire is the past, while Lord Sun is the next
If water is meeting, then lightning is negotiation
Know that this is the second Adhi-Jyoutisha for knowledge
If none of these happen, learning cannot happen |11|

Teacher is the past, while disciple is the next
If education is meeting, then preaching is negotiation

Know that this is the third Adhi-Vidya for knowledge
If none of these happen, education cannot happen |12|

Mother is the past, while father is the next
If a citizen is meeting, then a child is negotiation
Know that this is the fourth Adhi-Praja for knowledge
If none of these happen, education cannot happen |13|

The lower jaw is the past, while the upper jaw is the next
If speech is a meeting, then tongue is a negotiation
Know that this is the fifth Adhi-Atma for knowledge
If none of these happen, education cannot happen |14|

Every student should observe the five great codes
From this, he can obtain charisma, animals, and success
Only in this manner can one earn food and success
Otherwise, man cannot have heaven in the local process |15|

A student should ask the principal for knowledge
He should constantly chant Omkara, its seat for life
Omkara is the key to realizing the great Lord Brahman
But a person cannot realize this if his knowledge is common |16|

Please seek Lord Brahman to attain special knowledge
Practice the gain to see that it should not fade in bondage
If the intellectuality is not enough, the acquired wealth will go to waste
Applicable meaning must be sought in this world for the truth's grace |17|

A student should take refuge in Sri for all his wealth
He should pray for celibates to come to him
He should decide that I will take guidance from the quality of Dame
He should pray that those who come will have the quality of Shame |18|

A student should make sacrifices to be successful, honestly
He must hope that I want to be the richest among the rich
The student should ask, O Lord, I want to enter you
The student should ask, O Lord, please enter into me |19|

O Lord, I will wash away the dirt within me
O Lord, I will join you in pure love at the end
One should know that God is the resting place for oneself
knowing that this is impossible without understanding the inner self |20|

Bhuh, Bhuvaha, and Suvaha are the three types of Vyahrtis
Chamasa has observed that the fourth Vyahrti is Mahaha
A human being should understand that Mahaha is Brahman
All deities should be understood by humans as the Lord's organs |21|

Bhuh Bhuh Suvah Mahah Janah Tapah Satyam are the Vyahrtis
Because these will be pronounced in Agnihotra, etc., by Rishis
Man has to realize that this Brahman is the greatest in creation
One should know that the Lord is the great soul of cosmic lamination |22|

Along with this world, Agni and Rikku, pranas mean Bhuh
Along with space, air, and Sama, Apana means Bhuvah
Along with heaven, Aditya, Yajas, and Vyana mean Suvah
Moon, sun, Om, along with food, etc. mean Mahah |23|

Each Vyahrti is sixteen multiplied by four and four
Human beings have to worship them in these ways
These sixteen Vyahrti forms are to be understood as Brahman
As per the Upanishads, the Lord is the Shodasha Kala-purushan |24|

The vessel used in Soma yagas is called Chamasa
One who performs many Soma yagas is called Maha Chamasa
The secretion of the glands for awakening is the Soma Yaga of the Vedas
Chamasa is the one who awakens awareness within the four
consciousnesses|25|

The world we are in is Bhuh
The space we see is Bhuvah
If Suvah is the divine world, then Aditya is Mahah
From Aditya itself, all the worlds are enhanced |26|

The fire we use is Bhuh
The air we breathe is called Bhuvah
If Suvah is Aditya, Chandra is Mahah
All the lights are magnified by the moon itself |27|

Bhuhah is the actual Rikku in the Vedas
Bhuvah is the Samas mentioned in the Vedas
If Suva means Yajus, Brahma means Mahah
All the Vedas are enhanced by the Lord Brahman |28|

It is the Bhuh that we breathe
The apana that we have is Bhuvah
If suvah is vyana, food means mahah

All animals thrive on food in this world |29|

These Vyahrtis are divided into four parts
These lives are being followed in sixteen ways
Knowing these, one should know Brahman
For one who knows, the gods give oblation |30|

Within the hearts of beings is an opportunity
Manomaya Purusha is living in this cavity
A person is alive because of his flame vibrations
He observes every person's karmic intentions |31|

There is a sushumna between the two palates of the minor tongue
From there, it continues by penetrating the skull
For humans, it is the way to attain the Lord Brahman
A worshipper of God can get through it without confusion |32|

He who gains Brahma by worshipping him will stand in
Bhuha Agni, Bhuha Vayu, and Suvah Aditya in Maha Brahma
Such a person will have his own kingdom in this world with a mansion
And, he will become an eloquent, good listener, and scholarly person |33|

A worshipper who has earned it by worshipping Brahman
will actually earn a body in this world in a celestial manner
In addition, he will have a true soul, peace of mind, and happiness
In this way, the creatures here can become primitive with wellness |34|

In the Vedic style, there are five feet of Chandus
This is Pankta with the idea of the number five
Starting from the world to the soul, everything is Pankta
The form of Hiranyagarbha can be obtained from Pankta |35|

Earth, space, Dyuloka, direction, and Avantara are the world panktas
Fire, air, the sun, moon, and stars are the deity panktas
Water, plants, wood, sky, and soul are Bhuta Panktas
The worship of these panktas is the true sacrifice to the living being |36|

Wife, master, son, divine and human wealth Yajnya is Pankta
Along with Prana, Vyana, Apana, Udana, and Samana is air Pankta
Along with eyes, ears, mind, and speech, the skin is a sensory Pankta
Skin, meat, muscle, and bone, along with fat, are elements Pankta |37|

A Pankta should be completed from a pankta itself
All Yagnyas should be performed only with Pankta

As for the Yagnya, the spiritual is the same as the external norm
This is the only way for him to attain Hiranyagarbha form |38|

Omkara itself is a part of all kinds of worship on earth
Thus, there is advice from Vedic experts on the type of Ruta
Omkara should be worshipped with the view of Brahman here and there
Even though Omkara is only a sound, it gives Brahman for sure |39|

A celibate should acquire certain knowledge in his intellect
He should speak the truth only according to the cosmic order
Celibate should practice knowledge daily through their own study
On a regular basis, he should give discourses to the worldly |40|

Man can acquire his own kingdom through science
Thus, he should not abandon Shrauta and Smarta Karma
He should get the meaning of these from the god's head
He should see that karma is the means to manhood |41|

Discourse is most helpful, along with one's own study
Because knowledge of meaning depends on study
supreme merit depends on the meaning's righteousness
Actualities can be obtained through the practice of religiousness |42|

By intervening, I inspire the tree of worldly life
I will make the peak of my glory as high as a mountain
All this is easily possible for one who is in his soul form
For this, one has to keep his soul within the sun's norm |43|

Every man should speak the truth and practice his own religion
He should never make mistakes in his own studies
The money demanded by the teacher should be given to him
He should proceed with auspicious deeds with wisdom |44|

Man should not distract from his own studies and discourses
He should not be distracted by the works of his father and God
He should know that his parents are the gods of this world
Along with hospitality, he should honor the teacher in bold |45|

The prescribed karmas should be performed regularly
There should be speech only in good deeds, specifically
One should treat good people with the best seat, etc
It should be understood that Purusha Sanskara is from Shruti |46|

Abandon carelessness and practice diligence
One should give charity according to his wealth
Whatever you do, do it with humility, not in commotion
Diligence can only come from fear and true devotion |47|

Defective deeds practiced by the virtuous should be abandoned
Opposite deeds practiced by the teachers should be abandoned
Diligence should be developed by enduring hard work
One must perceive the essence in the company of the best |48|

There may be doubts about performing Shrauta and Smarta deeds
Dualities can be seen in terms of customs and ideas
Thus, one should inquire about everything and then proceed
Ask the Brahmins, who have a desire for righteousness, to succeed |49|

May Varuna, along with Mitra, bring us happiness
May Vayu, the manifest Brahman, bring us happiness
If Ruta is followed, the disciple will be comfortable with his teacher
If they pray for good men, then everything will go better |50|

Brahma Ananda Upasanam

May knowledge protect us both together
May education nurture us both together
When disciples pray like this, the guru and disciple will have ability together
Enmity will not arise between them when brilliance occurs together |1|

One who knows Brahman will possess Brahman itself
This sentence is an eternal truth in terms of Rita
This sentence that Brahma is truth-knowledge-infinity is true
All the inner desires of one who has Brahma will be fulfilled, for sure |2|

Brahma's truth is the form of not letting go after being determined
Brahman is not inert when truth is the true cause
Brahma knowledge is awareness, and it is not a doer, work, or deed
Because this knowledge has no end, it is infinite in cosmic need |3|

Opportunity was born from the soul, in the form of Brahma
If air was born from opportunity, fire was born from air
Water was born from fire, and solids from water for good
Food was born from solids, and potential was born from food |4|

Human organs are born from foods
Such a human being is full of juice from foods

The middle part of his body is the soul for him
He is standing from the lower part of the navel in firm |5|

Animals that shelter land are certainly born from food
These organisms live on food and eventually enter food
Hence, food is medicine for everything in common
So food should be worshipped as an eternal Brahman |6|

Those who worship food certainly will have food
They will know that food is the first of all elements
Everything is born from food as well as being eaten by it
It is said to be food because animals are being enriched by it |7|

There is one other than the soul, full of food juice
Inwardly, he is a soul full of air
This local food soul is filled with air
The soul itself is the form of potential in animals, in fair |8|

Life's potential is shaped by the soul, which is filled with food
Prana is the head, and Vyana is the south side of life
Apana is on the north side, and Samana is the centre of life
Animals on earth depend on the one who is filled with life |9|

Animals are living along with their senses, following the air
Life has been arranged for human beings, along with animals and birds
For this reason, this air is said to be the soul of all
One who worships it as Brahma gets full life in the local call |10|

A soul full of life is inside a body filled with food
There is someone else inside who is filled with life
He is nothing but a soul filled with mind
He is inside the body that is filled with wind |11|

Filled with mind, the soul is within in the form of potential
It became potent by following life's potential
The mind has Yajus as its head and Rik as its right side
Sama is mind's north, Brahman is its middle, and Atharva is its prestige |12|

Yajus is a profession of the innermost mind
The vocal effort through the tone of Nada is its feeling
Yajus of emotions are born through the instrument of hearing
Since mantras are the profession of the mind, they can be chanted with feeling|13|

A soul in a different form than the mind-filled soul is within
He is full of science, and he filled the soul of the mind within
By emulating the potential of the mind, science became potent within
Science is the determinate intellect that knows the meaning of the Vedas
within |14|

Diligence is the head of a soul filled with knowledge
\Cosmic order is the south, and truth is the north for him
If yoga is the medium, Mahat principle is prestige for him
The character of study and practice is his interim |15|

Atman, filled with science, is the product of a deterministic form of science
Diligence, etc., in duty will be born from the product of science
Through diligence, etc., awareness of the principle is born in samadhi
The soul filled with science is the yoga that occurs in Samadhi |16|

He who knows the soul of science performs the Yagnya diligently
For this reason, even the eternal gods worship science silently
Science should be worshipped as the supreme Brahman
Desires become reality only when sins are abandoned |17|

There is another soul within than the science-filled soul
This science soul exists from that bliss-filled soul
If beloved is his head, the Moda is the right side
If Pramoda is on the left, happiness is in the middle |18|

This blissful being is not Brahman but only the soul of action
Because, according to the sage, it is sub-transcending the soul
Since this bliss is worship, it is the fruit of karma
This blissful soul is the disfiguration of the fruits of karma |19|

This bliss is nothing but the soul of action
If a being sees its liking things, it will feel happiness
Happiness is born from the acquisition of desirable things
If joy became high, this would become bliss for beings |20|

This Brahman is the form of bliss along with truth and knowledge
To realize its knowledge, there is a teaching of five koshas
This eternal Brahman within all is the soul of all koshas
Non-dual Brahman is the bliss that is there to transcend duality |21|

Sat means Brahman is present, and Asat means he is absent
The one who says no means that potential has nothing to do with him

Whoever says that he exists will get the true form of Brahman
It means that those who have preached this know Brahman |22|

If Sat means good while Asat means bad
Asat means that person is not diligent on the right path
Sat means a person is devoted to the Lord, the eternal Brahman
One should know that all teachers have preached like this to humans' |23|

Asat objects are not the real cause of the present world
Brahman alone can be known as the cause of the world
Brahman willed only to create, but he is a truly listless person
This world is only for the fruit of karma and not for the benefit of Brahman|24|

Brahman, without organs, is not multiplicity, along with the diminutive
Thus doing penance, Lord, eternal Brahman contemplated creation
These sages saw that knowledge is penance in this world
Hence, Lord Brahman contemplated the creation of this world |25|

This knowledge of Brahman is divisive and natural
To know his form, it is said about the koshas' factual
One should understand the saying 'Yo Veda Nihita Guhayam'
This eternal Brahman is infinite with truth and knowledge |26|

There is a Brahman entrance into a cave filled with science
Filled with bliss, he dwells in it with a unique form and pace
Through Linga, Brahman's glory and dignity should be understood
Along with his immutability, one should realize the existence of mutability |27|

Brahman is un-manifest because it has no special quality in actualization
There is awareness of that Braman through special object relations
Brahman is realized only through the inner apparatus
Brahman manifests in the form of a seer, a hearer, a teller, and a knower |28|

If the tangible is Satt, this abstract is Asatt
Within the soul, these have one name and one form
These are different from the immanent soul
The soul becomes these two by manifesting itself |29|

Descriptive and indescribable are tangible and intangible features
Descriptive means to explain that the substance classified by equal, unequal,
caste, substance, and combined by space and time is this and that
The opposite is always indescribable of that |30|

Shelter is a characteristic of the embodiment form
The opposite is the characteristic of the abstract norm
Science means one who has spirit, according to the Vedas
Non-scientific means inert, and these are divisional adjectives |31|

This figurative world with an adjective was Asatt first
Later, it became Satt from the incorporeal Brahman
Names and forms were produced by the eternal Brahman
In this Brahman is the juice that causes satisfaction |32|

That Brahman is the juice of bliss in life on our part
Its real acceptance is in the celestial intellect of the heart
If this bliss is not there, then how is the movement of life possible?
Impunity can be attained only by giving up the concept of 'I' |33|

Even the slightest difference in the vision of Brahmn is not good
A hollow scholar does not get the taste of non-duality
A scholar with duality is always afraid of this world
Even such a wise scholar is ignorant and has no hold |34|

The wind blows for the true bliss of Brahman
The sun will rise, and fire will also work
Indra will work for this pleasure without stopping
The fifth god, called death, runs without stopping |35|

A human being should know the idea of blissfulness
He should understand bliss in comparison, stage by stage
The bliss of a very efficient person is the bliss of man
The bliss of such a hundred men is the bliss of one Shrotriya |36|

The bliss of a Shrotriya is the bliss of a human Gandharva
Hundred human Gandharva bliss is the bliss of one Deva-Gandharva
Deva Gandharva's bliss is the bliss of a desireless Shrotriya
Hundred Deva Gandharva's bliss is the bliss of one Pitru |37|

The bliss of a Pitru is the bliss of a desireless shrotriya
The bliss of a hundred Pitru is the bliss of one karmic deity
The bliss of a karmic deity is the bliss of a Shrotriya
Hundred karmic deities' bliss is the bliss of a god who receives an offering |38|

The bliss of a god who receives an offering is the bliss of a shrotriya
The bliss of these hundred gods is the bliss of Lord Indra
The bliss of a lord, Indra, is the bliss of a Shrotriya
Hundred Indra's bliss is the bliss of a Bruhaspati |39|

The bliss of a Bruhaspati is the bliss of a shrotriya
The bliss of these hundred Bruhaspatis is the bliss of Prajapati
The bliss of a Prjapati is the bliss of a Shrotriya
Hundred Prajapati's bliss is the bliss of a Brahma |40|

He who is in Purusha and in Aditya alone,
He who is in the sky of the heart alone,
He who has created and entered into it is Brahman
Whoever realizes him in the koshas becomes the Brahman |41|

From which the word returns without matching the mind,
He who realizes the bliss of that Brahman fears nothing
Such a person will never be caught between sin and virtue
Having nullified everything, he became a hero by nature |42|

Bhrugu Upasanam

Bhrigu asked Varuna, O Deva, please teach me Brahman
Varuna told him to know food, prana, sight, hearing, mind, and speech
First, one must know what the creation consists of and where it belongs
Immediately after knowing this, Bhrigu went to penance to know Brahman |1|

Animals will be borne by food, live by it, and finally enter the food
So Bhrigu, realizing that this is Brahma, saw the production of food
Suspicious, he again asked Varuna what Brahma is
He was sent by Varuna to know Brahma through penance |2|

Animals will be borne by Prama, live by it, and finally enter the Prana
So Bhrigu, realizing that this is Brahma, saw the production of Prana
Suspicious, he again asked Varuna what Brahma is
He was sent by Varuna to know Brahma through penance |3|

Animals will be borne by the mind, live by it, and finally enter the mind
So Bhrigu, realizing that this is Brahma, saw the production of mind
Suspicious, he again asked Varuna what Brahma is
He was sent by Varuna to know Brahma through penance |4|

Animals will be borne by science, live by it, and finally enter science
So Bhrigu, realizing that this is Brahma, saw the production of science
Suspicious, he again asked Varuna what Brahma is
He was sent by Varuna to know Brahma through penance |5|

Animals will be borne by bliss, live by it, and finally enter bliss
So Bhrigu, realizing that this is Brahma, saw the bliss in the cosmos

Then Bhrigu became enshrined in truth-knowledge-infinite Brahma
Along with food, Bhrigu became a great sage due to God's charisma |6|

No one should abuse food, as it is the door to knowledge of Brahman
As food is life to the body, it should be worshipped by humans
One who realizes that this food is prestigious becomes a giver of food
Thus, he becomes glorified by the charisma of Brahma for good |7|

Food should not be denied; water is also food; illumination is to give food
illumination in water and water in illumination is established
One who realizes that this food is prestigious becomes a giver of food
Thus, he becomes glorified by the charisma of Brahma for good |8|

Food should be multiplied; the earth is also food; the sky is to give food
Earth in the sky and sky in the earth are established
One who realizes that this food is prestigious becomes a giver of food
Thus, he becomes glorified by the charisma of Brahma for good |9|

Welcome guests who are at the door; that is the real ceremony
If one donates food, he will get high fruits in harmony
Charity should be done at an early, middle, and late age
Treat hospitality as the worship of food as a privilege |10|

Worship should be done as health in speech, as well-being in life,
deeds in the hands, and movement in the feet
Every man should actually worship the Brahman that is in the air
And one should realize that all these are worships of human affairs |11|

It should be worshipped as satisfaction in rain, strength in lightning,
success in animals, and illumination in stars
Within us is the bliss of procreation and immortality
The worship of Brahma is the worship of the gods in mortality |12|

If the sky is worshipped as prestige, man becomes prestigious
If it is worshipped as Mahat, he becomes Mahat
If the sky is worshipped as the mind, man becomes capable of thinking
If he worships it with a salute, he will get indulgent things upon waking |13|

If the sky is worshipped as Brahman, man will attain Brahman
If it is worshipped as an instrument of destruction, the enemies will be
destroyed
In lightning, rain, the moon, the sun, fire, and the sky, humans will merge
If it is worshipped as Brahman, the path of achievement becomes easy with an
urge |14|

He who is in Aditya with Purusha is none other than Atman
One who knows this leaves this world and joins the food Atman
Then he joins life, mind, science, and bliss Atman
He sings Sama in this world, attaining all fortune as a human |15|

Hey! Hey! Hey! I am the food, I am the giver of food, I am the creator
of the verse, I am born before this material-immaterial world, I am the
first of the group of gods, the imperishable, that good one will exclaim
He will also declare that he will save this world through righteousness |16|

Code of Conduct

Before doing any work, one should remember God
See, the sages ate the crop grown by that Lord
That eternal divine power is there for every work
With that, work proceeds unhindered, brick by brick |1|

Vedic Sutras should be followed diligently
Every task should be done perfectly
Before executing, the negative effects should be observed
If there is no haste, things will be done with pure essence |2|

One should know what profit is and loss is
A code of conduct should actually be implemented
These are to facilitate making the right decision
This will generate an adequate flow of precision |3|

No one should ever give advice to a fool
No one should support a misguided woman
Suffering is unavoidable for the misadventure man
If something is negative, it should be avoided with a plan |4|

In which house there is a woman who speaks badly,
in which house there is a servant who talks too much
that house will become like hell on a daily basis
For good, ugly ones should be shunned without kindness |5|

Money should be saved for real emergencies
Saved money should be used for women's protection
Yes, one should lead a life of sacrifice and gratification
But selfishness is right when it comes to protection |6|

Before doing anything, think properly
Do the work calmly and mindfully
Whoever does not speak about the work is always the best
If there is no bragging, the work will not be that difficult |7|

A person's idiocy and stupidity bring him trouble
To be angry in youth will bring him much trouble
Living in someone else's house is more difficult than either of these
If one does not get out of these three, his life will certainly freeze |8|

Gems are not found in all the mountains of the world
Good people are not found in all parts of the world
Not everyone gets everything in one life as one wishes
Everything happens according to the calculation of sins and merits |9|

Parents should make their children healthy
Punctuality should be taught along with food
One should teach restraint to reach goals to their children
If the children succeed, so will the grandchildren |10|

Education is very important in this competitive world
There are many subjects about it, even from Vedic times
Wisdom and ingenuity are like a crown for one's norm
One who realizes this will make a name on a global forum |11|

Love, discipline, and restraint are very important for a student
Excessive affection is very dangerous for any child
Any person can learn from situations in the world
If one does not realize this, he becomes useless in his mould |12|

Students should be busy with their studies every day
They should pay attention to practice every day
The habit of mindless reading is like pouring rain on stone
Knowledge is always a powerful weapon in this social zone |13|

Insult from the relatives is equivalent to serving an evil boss
Debt, along with poverty, is like a pain in the hips
Working under an unhappy boss is very difficult
Such a life is like keeping fire inside a garment |14|

The tree on the bank of the river will surely perish
The life of a woman living in another's house is painful
Such is the condition of a king with foolish ministers
All their lives will surely be destroyed in every cluster |15|

Knowledge is the wealth of Brahmins
A strong army is the wealth of a king
Business people should know that money is wealth
Others should know that service is their wealth |16|

A harlot will turn away the penniless
A defeated king is rejected by the subjects
Birds do not live on a tree that never bears fruit
The one who does not know these secrets will be ruined |17|

The moment the work is done, it is better to leave
It is best to leave the moment the study is over
Otherwise, the rest may suffer because of one's manners
Life becomes difficult for those who do not know manners |18|

Good friends hope for prosperity forever
A good environment strives for one's prosperity
Choose good friends carefully for the sake of good pace
It is true that the company of the wicked disturbs the peace |19|

Friendship should only be with equals
Association should only be with the truly wise
By this, one's personality blossoms without doubt
A wise woman is a good sign for any house |20|

Where is the faultless clan in this world?
Where is the man in this world who does not get sick?
There is no person who is not at risk from bad habits
Happiness every day is a mirage in this world |21|

A person's actions indicate his refinement strength
The style of speech tells about his place of birth
The words will show a person's innermost being
The diet can be known from his body's framing |22|

It is the duty of a householder to get a daughter into a good family
It is his responsibility to give proper education to the children
One's trick is to make the enemy addicted to bad habits
Hiring a good friend for good work shows a good habit |23|

Choose the serpent between the serpent and the wicked
A serpent bites only in defense
But this evil person will sting without reason
It is wise to stay away from such people in person |24|

Always put the wise in your counsel
They will solve your problems in difficult times
Their role in victory and defeat is huge in your career
You will never receive a favor from just a praiser |25|

The sea crosses the boundary in a storm
It completely immerses the house's' form
Thus, one should not lose inner composure in calamities
For this, the lives of the sages should be thoroughly scrutinized |26|

Without refinements, man would be inferior to an animal
Therefore, they do not sit idly in the company of good people
Nobody likes someone who will create irritation
The world has to be won over by good participation |27|

No one wants a flower without fragrance
No one likes him if he has no rites
One should be well-educated, even if he comes from a poor family
Then he can live with respect and honor in this world, firmly |28|

A sweet voice is the ornament of a cuckoo
For a cultured woman, her body is the jewel
Education is beauty for the ugly rage
Forgiveness is the ornament to Sage |29|

To bring good to the house, cast out the evil person within
If it is good for the village, throw out a bad clan from within
Abandon a village if it pleases the local people
If you want to attain liberation, leave this world |30|

One who is engaged in employment never has to fear poverty
One who is engaged in penance is never afraid of sin
Whoever is in perpetual silence never has a quarrel
Whoever is ever vigilant has no fears in aural |31|

Sita was faced worse by her excessive beauty
Excessive pride led to Ravana's downfall
Emperor Bali was also drowned by excessive charity
Even from all sides, it is good to leave this excess for clarity |32|

Nothing is impossible for the strong
Nothing is too far for a farmer
No country is a stranger when it comes to acquiring an education
No one is new until they are spoken to with love and affection |33|

The fragrant tree fills the entire forest with fragrance
The son will light up the clan with his good behavior
Only five Pandavas are wiser than 101 Kauravas
Chanakya also holds the same opinion on his nose |34|

A fire that touches a dead tree can burn an entire forest
One wicked son can destroy an entire clan
There is no better example of this than Duryodhana
It is the duty of parents to give sanskram to their children |35|

The waxing moon dispels darkness
A wise son will bring happiness to the house
Always, success is ideal for the world's coolers
This is also the inner desire of Vedic scholar's |36|

Babies should be pampered for the first five years
They should be punished for the next ten years
In sixteen years, they should be seen as allies
And parents should expand their children's streams of thought |37|

When one feels that it is no longer appropriate to be there,
he should immediately leave that place
One has to leave one's own village in extreme rains and droughts
Otherwise, one will get stuck with material problems |38|

One should realize the four types of Purushartha in reality
With religion, prosperity, and deeds, one should have faith in salvation
These four ideas are the pillars of Indian culture
This makes mental as well as physical trading easier |39|

Where true gentlemen are honored,
Where food grains are safe,
There, Sri Lakshmi stays with honor
There, people don't fight each other |40|

What a Yogi gets is for a Yogi, and what a Jogi gets is for a Jogi
What has been earned in the previous life will come to the bag of this birth
Whether one is a Yogi or a Jogi is decided by the womb's mention
Death is predetermined along with age, karma, wealth, and education |41|

Mythology is an integral part of our Indian culture
But while listening to these, our focus is on other matters
There is salvation for one in listening to moral stories
These are the guiding lights in difficult-time memories |42|

Saints tell us how one should live morally
Also tells how to deal with here-and-there ideas
These speeches of saints are very useful for life
This creates a ray of hope in one's life's strife |43|

Who knows when death will come and cover?
Who gives time when that bloody death is near?
Therefore, when strong, one should perform good activities
One should know that good deeds cannot be done when weak |44|

Like Kamadhenu, education and scholarship can give everything
These can save men both at home and abroad
Education and scholarship can earn respect and dignity
An example of this is ancient India, which had a Gurus with clarity |45|

Living in a bad village, serving evil people,
having poor food, having a grumpy wife-
all these things lead to hell for a man every day
A widowed daughter will generate grief in every play |46|

What is the use of a cow that does not give milk?
What is the use of a son who is not devoted to God?
What is the use of living without knowing the purpose of birth?
What is the use of just eating without doing anything worth? |47|

There are a few things that bring comfort to a sad local life
A good son and a good soul mate bring coolness to life
Good human associations are needed by everyone in life
An oceanic ratio of sadness to happiness is sure in one's life |48|

A king commands only once
Scholars speak only once
According to practice, a daughter can marry only once
In real life, everyone gets only one good chance |49|

Work that requires concentration should be done in solitude
Two students should learn the subject together because of its magnitude
There should be three for the completeness of musical practice
One should know how many people should be involved in each task |50|

Any family without offspring is void
The life of a person without relatives is like a void
A fool without feelings is like an inert object
The life of a poor person is like a dry subject |51|

Learning without practice is toxic
Food is most poisonous when sick
This society is poisonous to the poor
A young wife is poisonous to an old man |52|

A religion that does not teach love-kindness should be abandoned
After realizing the knowledge, one should leave that teacher
There is never happiness from a grumpy wife
Unloving relatives should be shunned without grief |53|

A person who is always travelling will grow old quickly
A horse that is tied all the time will get old very quickly
Clothes left to dry in the sun will deteriorate quickly
Youthfulness should be preserved for daily activity |54|

How is time treating me?
How many true friends do I have?
There should be details about the living location
This focus is the true mark of a wise man |55|

The father who gives birth, the priest who performs the worship,
A teacher who teaches knowledge, a parent who protects,
It should be realized that all of them are equal to the father
If you forget them, there will be no progress in life further |56|

King's wife and teacher's wife,
Friend's wife and wife's mother,
One should consider them equal to his mother
If you forget them, there will be no development further |57|

Agni is the teacher for Brahmins
Brahmana is the teacher for all colors
For a wife, her husband is her teacher
The guest is the teacher in all manners |58|

Gold is tested by scratching, cutting, heating, and piercing
The nature of a person is known through words and intellect
Good qualities can test one's personality
One's heart shows their true loyalty |59|

It is useless to think about the unpleasant incidents of the past
There is no use worrying about what will happen next
When problems are encountered, one should think of elimination
The wise see everything with equanimity to attain resolution |60|

The fruits of the tree vary in size and taste
Children born to the same mother are different
Everything In creation has its own original form
Self-parameters are responsible for these different norms |61|

Those in power are less likely to walk with sincerity
A fool to play sweet talks is little in this world
A good lover adorns himself with the suit
Those who do not cover themselves do not cheat |62|

Fools get jealous when they see scholars
The poor get jealous when they see the rich
Harlots eat bitterness when they see a happy couple
None of them will develop without giving up this evil shuffle |63|

Laziness spoils academic practice
Sowing a little seed spoils a whole field
A woman who has gone to another man will be completely ruined
The death of an army officer will make the entire army blind |64|

Studying becomes successful with systematic daily practice
The family will be blessed by its religious activities
A wise person is distinguished by his noble qualities
Eyes will show a man's inner anger in many ways |65|

Religion is protected by money
Knowledge is protected by yoga
Soft language protects the kings
A good housewife protects her member's |66|

Charity and religion eradicate poverty
Good qualities drive away suffering
True knowledge will remove the ignorance
Devotion to God will eliminate inner fears |67|

There is no other disease equal to lust
There is no other enemy equal to infatuation
There is no fire equal to anger's kiss
With knowledge comes the realization of bliss |68|

Man comes alone to this world of ours
According to his karma, he will participate alone
Eventually he will go to heaven alone with karmic feeds
In this world, no one is responsible for anyone's deeds |69|

To one who knows Brahman, this heaven is negligible
This life is nothing for a brave warrior
A woman is nothing to one who has conquered the senses
To one who overcomes desires, this world is not an expense |70|

Knowledge is the friend of the traveler
A good wife is a friend to her master
Medicine becomes a true friend when you are sick
At the time of death, charity and religion become friend's |71|

The rain that falls into the sea is wasted
On a full stomach, food is wasted
If charity is given to a rich person, it will be wasted
If you light a lamp during the day, it will be wasted |72|

There is no other water that is purer than the cloud
There is no other power like the power of the soul
There is no other brilliance equal to the eyes
There is no other thing as dear as grain |73|

He who has no money wants money
Dumb animals want the power of speech
Human beings desire heaven
The eternal gods seek salvation |74|

This truth is what keeps the Earth in its orbit
Truth gives light from the sun
The truth is what makes the wind blow
This world proceeds with truth's flow |75|

Money comes, then goes
Prana comes, then goes
Life also comes and goes
Dharma alone will stand here forever |76|

A barber is the wisest of men
The crow is the wisest of birds
Foxes are the most cunning of animals
A flower seller is wise among females |77|

If one listens to the scriptures, he can understand their secrets
If one listens to discourse, bad thoughts will go away
So, for the sake of knowledge, one should seek the initiation
Then, everyone can walk on the path of salvation |78|

The crow is the meanest of birds
A dog is the meanest of animals
A short-tempered sage is bad
Whoever abuses behind one's back is bad |79|

Ashes make the vessel clean
Copper is purified by lemon
Menstruation cleanses a woman
Due to the fast flow, the river becomes clean |80|

A king who roams the kingdom will be adored
Scholars who lecture in other countries will be respected
Monks travelling around the country should be respected
A woman in the house should be cherished |81|

A rich man always has lots of relatives
He is worshipped daily by many friends
Money should not come between relatives
Everyone should give a seat to true scholar's |82|

Time swallows all beings
Time will kill all people
No one in this world can surpass the potential of time
When everything is asleep, only time will be awake |83|

A person born blind cannot see anything
One who is blinded by lust cannot see anything
One who is mad with ego sees nothing
A selfish person is more blind than anyone else |84|

This man will be born in this local world
He gets stuck in the cycle and experiences everything
One has to eat the fruits of his own deeds
Take refuge in God and escape from this circle of deeds |85|

The king must eat the fruits of the people's sins
The fruit of the king's sin must be eaten by his priest
The fruit of the wife's sin must be eaten by her master
The fruit of the student's sin must be eaten by his teacher |86|

The enemy is the father, who puts his son in debt
The enemy is the mother who lost virtue
A beautiful wife is the enemy of a husband
A stubborn son is the real enemy of his parent's |87|

Greed can be conquered by the power of money
Pride can be won by bowing down with honey
Listening can win over a fool
A pandit can be won over only by telling the truth |88|

It is better to have none than a bad kingdom
It is better not to have them than to have evil friends
A bad student should not be taught a lesson consistently
A wicked wife should be put away immediately |89|

People are not happy under the rule of an evil king
A bad friend is of no use to any human being
A husband is not happy with a wicked wife
Teaching a stupid student is worse than any strife |90|

One should hunt like a lion in the forest
The vision should be focused, like a bird
To achieve the goal, one should have this platform
One should have concentration while performing |91|

One should wake up early, like a hen
In war, one must know offensive-defensiveness
An equal share of the labor should be given to the family
Good will happen to the one who realizes these principles firmly |92|

Don't put too much trust in anyone
Food which is not available in emergencies is of no use
Everyone should be vigilant in this world
Good will happen to the one who realizes these moulds |93|

A dog will eat well when food is available
If food is not available, then it sleeps without worrying
If there is any noise in sleep, the dog wakes up immediately
One who realizes these qualities in a dog will live happily |94|

Without calculation, a donkey works tirelessly
It carries the burden entrusted to it, silently
Indefatigable work is the true quality of a donkey
One should learn that one should work without being annoying |95|

Man has much to learn from birds
He has much to learn from animals
One should learn the lesson by looking at nature
One who does this will succeed in the future |96|

One should not shy away from business and enterprise
One should be upright while learning about the subject
Being not shy in business will be profitable
Those who know no when they feel no can be happy |97|

No one should go after money
One should not over-crave for riches
One should be satisfied with what one gets
Only then will the mind be calm without being nuts |98|

One should be satisfied with the wife and children obtained
\One should be satisfied with income and business
But don't be satisfied with studying and gaining knowledge
Only then will the observance of duty not go astray in this bondage |99|

A layman should not talk between two scholars
No one should come between the fire and the priests
Do not stand between husband and wife and talk
If not done inappropriately, life is as beautiful as a good walk |100|

One should not touch Agni and the priest by feet
One should not touch teachers and Brahmins by feet
No one should touch a mother cow with their feet
It is a crime to touch these venerable ones with your feet |101|

One should be five cubits away from the bullock cart
One should be ten cubits away from the horse
One should be a thousand cubits away from the elephant
If there is an evil person, that area should be left |102|

An elephant can be controlled by a goad
A horse can be controlled by hands
A stick is enough to control cattle
But a sword is needed to control evil |103|

A brahmin who sees the food becomes happy
Seeing the clouds, the peacock raises its feathers
Gentlemen rejoice in seeing the fortunes of others
A wicked man rejoices in the sufferings of others |104|

A strong enemy should be overcome with grace
A weak enemy should be met with swank
An equal enemy should be viewed in context
When and how to walk should be learned by text |105|

The prowess of the shoulder is the jewel of the king
Knowledge is the true adornment of a Brahmin
Along with beauty, virtue is an ornament for a woman
By doing so, they will have happiness as humans |106|

A straightforward nature should never be developed
Because upright trees will be cut down first!
An ugly man is always safe with his local pals
Because this world is full of ugly pitfalls |107|

As long as there is water in the lake, swans will stay
Deer graze as long as there is green in the forest
But humans should not be changing places like this
Instead, they should build a town where there is |108|

Prosperity must be earned with hard work
Earnings should be saved for bad times
Wealth should be used only for good deeds
Because running water will maintain cleanliness |109|

A person with money has more relatives and friends
Only those who have money have respect and property
Only those who have money have status in society
Earning money can lead to a happy life filled with prosperity |110|

Donors are always like those eternal gods
Those who believe in God are like angels
The humble one should be treated with respect
The good ones should be treated with great respect |111|

Harsh-talking people are always bad
Those who are hostile to their own people are bad
Never trust a mean person
Because hell will be created by them |112|

The company of gentlemen tastes like honey
The company of bad people Is like a bee sting
One should always be in the company of dignitaries
One should stay away from the company of meaner's |113|

What good is it for a dog to have a tail?
Because it is unable to repel mosquitoes
There is a saying that little knowledge is great pride
So, one must have thorough knowledge of his field |114|

A good word from a pure heart,
a good word played with pure character,
kindness shown in animals is good motivation
He who has these good qualities is the official for salvation |115|

The scent is invisible in the flower
The oil is invisible in sesame seed
The soul is invisible in the body's stardom
Atman can be realized through wisdom |116|

Mean-minded people only desire money
Mediums ask for respect as well as money
The good ones give favors along with respect
More important than wealth are prestige and respect |117|

There is no need for any kind of law for worship
It is not wrong to eat and then worship
Medicine can be consumed and then worshipped
However, the rules should not exceed Vedic kinship |118|

A lamp swallows darkness and produces light
Eating the right food brings good thoughts
The mind moves according to the delicacy of the food
According to the food consumed, one creates his own kid |119|

O God, give riches to the good
Make them use it for good
The mass of water in the sea is not fit for drinking
There is no use in giving money for greedy thinking |120|

One should take a bath after applying the oil
A bath should be taken while attending the funeral
A bath is necessary to remove dirt as well as germs
Elders have said the usefulness of bathing with terms |121|

Water is medicine for indigestion
Drinking water revitalizes all organs
Drinking water before going to bed can prevent heart attacks
Drinking water after meals is forbidden after checking the facts |122|

If the spouse passes away in old age,
All the accumulated wealth goes to the relatives,
If he becomes a parasite even for dinner, it will be bad luck
A helpless man is truly unfortunate on life's check |123|

The study of the Vedas without sacrifices is not correct
Yagnya-yaga without charity and dharma is not right
Devotional spirit is the source of the Dharmic chain
If the Lord is not pleased, everything done is in vain |124|

Shiva, as a yogi, is in tune with devotees moods
Hari is a philosophical yogi, as his devotees note
By invoking the Lord in the idol, the worship becomes meaningful
Acharya's saying ``Yadbhavam Tadbhavati'' is so wonderful |125|

This Lord is not in the idols of stone or wood
But he is in the heart of every human being
Emotions in the mind are important in worship
All the scriptures of the world enrich this kinship. |126|

There is no penance equal to peace
There is no happiness greater than contentment
There is no other disease than wantingness
There is no religion other than kindness |127|

Anger inside is like death
The burning thirst for wealth is like a river
Education gives everything to every local being
Contentment is true happiness for a human being |128|

Quality is an ornament to beauty
Virtue is an ornament for the clan
For practice, achievement is an ornament.
For money, indulgence is an ornament |129|

Without quality, beauty will be destroyed
Bad qualities will destroy the clan itself
If there is no achievement, education will perish
If there are no spenders, money will perish |130|

The water that springs from the earth is pure
A good wife is a true friend to her husband
The great king is the one who does the welfare work
A contented Brahmin is holy in this local bark |131|

An unhappy brahmin's life will be ruined
In the kingdom of a contented king, there is only sorrow
A shy prostitute will not attract somebody's dad
The life of an unscrupulous housewife is only sad |132|

No one is superior or inferior by birth
A good clan is of no use if there is no education
No one even notices the caste of the rite-bearer
Respect is not due to caste or clan, which is clear |133|

Society suffers from alcoholics
Meat eaters are a thorn in this society
What does one expect from people who are like animals?
The cause of this crisis is the lack of true rites |134|

A Yagnya that destroys grains is useless
Yagna performed without the mantras is useless
There is no use of sacrifice without charity
Meaningless ritual is the enemy of society |135|

For liberation, one must give up lust, anger, infatuation, and greed
Instead, forgiveness, simplicity, purity, and truth should be celebrated
As the saying goes, ``Sarva Bhuta Hite Ratah'' should wish good
Attaining salvation is not easy for any being in this world |136|

Do not criticize relatives and friends' own affairs
One should not risk his life by crossing this line
Those who do not know this will harm themselves
It is like a serpent entering the anthill without knowing its secrets |137|

That creator did not put perfume in gold
He did not put the fruit inside the sugarcane
A wise person never becomes rich
No one can know the essence of that God much |138|

Honey is important in all medicines
Food is the greatest of all comforts
Eyes are the most important of all senses
The head is the most important of all the organs |139|

Messengers do not travel in the sky
No news is broadcast beforehand
Brahmins are aware of solar-lunar eclipses in advance
There is nothing in our world other than knowledge of penance |140|

A sleeping student should be knocked and warned
Also, the servant, traveler, and treasurer should be warned
A gatekeeper should be alert, along with the frightened
No one should forget the duties and responsibilities of the trend |141|

No one should wake the sleeping serpent
A king, a tiger, a dog, and a fool should not be alarmed
Because the one who warns them will surely be harmed
No one should forget this idea in their life |142|

It is the duty of a Brahmin to study the eternal Vedas
It is forbidden for him to demand food from an ugly person
We should not give ourselves up for money sake
If they do, they will be as useless as a non-venomous snake |143|

Even if there is no venom, it should be shrill like a snake
Justice should be done without causing any injustice
These characteristics should be natural in humans
Otherwise, no one can walk on the path of religion |144|

Wise people should listen to the Mahabharata in the morning
They should read the Ramayana at midday
The wise should recite the Bhagavata at night, as nature
See, Ramayana-Mahabharata-Bhagavata is our culture |145|

A necklace made with one's own hands will be best
The sandal that is produced with one's hands will be the best
Verses woven with originality will be best
These are more than the beauty of Indra, at least |146|

Arrows become sharper as they are sharpened
Gold shines more if one rubs it more
By sowing, the earth will yield in bulk
An unpolished intellect is like a dog's milk |147|

Poverty can be removed if one is courageous
Old clothes shine definitely with cleanliness
By heating food better taste can be recovered
By the good qualities, the ugliness can be covered |148|

One is not poor just because he does not have wealth
A wealthy man without education is never rich
In this reality, education is real wealth
To get knowledge, one must try with good health |149|

One should walk carefully
Drink only filtered water
These Shastras say that one should speak gently
Work should be done to make everyone happy regularly |150|

One who wants happiness in life should leave education
Whoever desires knowledge should renounce happiness
Whoever pursues happiness will not learn anything wisely
One should learn and know the subject very deeply |151|

Poets observe everything
Women do everything
Only drunks will tell everything
Crows also eat everything |152|

If God wills, He can make the rich poor
He can make a king a beggar if he wishes
In one's salvation, God will abduct all without kindness
Otherwise, how can renunciation come in happiness? |153|

For a greedy person, a beggar is an enemy
For a fool, an advisor is an enemy
For prostitutes, their husband is an enemy
 For thieves, a good moonlit night is the enemy |154|

There should be the qualities of learning, austerity, etc
To attain this, one has to give up his animal career
Friendship means living in harmony with the environment
Otherwise, this man will be lower than animals in the present |155|

No wood can become sandal by the wind blowing from the Malaya mountains
No admonition has any effect on one who has impurity in his intentions
Keeping the mind and heart pure is true humanity
Otherwise, this man will become lower than animals |156|

There is no way to make evil good
No matter how much you clean the anus, it doesn't get clean
One has to realize his pollution and fix it
Otherwise, happiness in this world is impossible, mind it |157|

No Shastra can correct a mindless person
A blind man does not see any benefit from a mirror
If this intellect is not ripe, everything in the world is in vain
If one is not washed by rites, his own principles go in vain |158|

If he hates his soul, he will die
If he hates others, he will not gain wealth
If one hates the king, he will be destroyed
If a brahmin is hated, the clan will be destroyed |159|

Better is the life of one who lives in a tree in the forest, or
by eating yams and drinking the water of the river,
than living without money among relatives
If you don't earn money, life in your own home will be difficult |160|

The root of the brahna tree is sandhyavandan
If Veda is its branch, Dharma and Karma are its leaves
So everyone should protect the source in a proper manner
Otherwise, the tree will wither and the leaves will disappear |161|

Where the parents are Narayana-Lakshmi
and their relatives are present as devotees,
the three worlds become their abodes
They can do this with good codes |162|

He who is born must die, and he who dies must be born
One should realize that this is a cycle of creation
No man should mourn for this because it is a credit
These occur only in the form of the attachment of debt |163|

Human intellect is more powerful than anything else
One's determination is stronger than anything else
Without these powers, everything is a waste
It is just a mirage for him that I will grow with taste |164|

This god carries all the burdens of the world
He is the one who is giving everything to living lives
Knowing this, why is it human to worry about life?
The one who surrenders to God will move without strife |165|

One should love languages, including the mother tongue
One should know their special features
After knowing the language, one should understand its breadth
Everything in the world should be learned by covering its depths |166|

Flour contains ten times more energy than rice
Milk has ten times more energy than flour
Meat is ten times more powerful than milk
Ghee has ten times more energy than meat |167|

Health becomes good through clean food
Consuming milk increases one's nutrition
Consumption of ghee increases sperm count
By consuming the meat, inertia will mount. |168|

Along with virtue and bravery,
Daring, along with sweet talk,
All these cannot be acquired through feeds
Instead, they come from birth due to deeds |169|

Inherited religion should not be sold for any reason
No person should leave his own people and settle elsewhere
If so, he will be the cause of his own destruction
One can see those who were destroyed in the path of iniquity selection |170|

An elephant can be controlled by a sharp edge
A lamp drives away the thick darkness
Hardness can be shredded with a diamond punch
That which is filled with brilliance is strong, but not size |171|

A student who is homesick does not get an education
A meat eater will never have mercy
A greedy person never has knowledge of truth or falsity
For Sybarite, sanctity never comes to his clarity |172|

At the end of 10,000 years, Vishnu will leave the earth
At the end of 5,000 years, Ganga will leave the earth
At the end of 2,500 years, the goddess will abandon the village
All this happens because religions are reckoned with God |173|

Fools never change, even if advised many times
Even if taught in many ways, evil people will never change
If honey is poured into the Neem tree, its bitterness does not leave
A human being can never change his fundamental nature |174|

Even if one bathes in a shrine, his inner being will not become pure
Even if alcohol vessels are burned, they will not be clean
Anything done without this pure inner being is in vain
Only through rites does one's inner being become pure and shine |175|

Those who do not know the qualities will always abuse them
Those who do not know the qualities will abuse even God
Jealousy is the source of many criticisms, as one can detect
There is no medicine in this world for this nature defect |176|

A man should be silent while eating food
One should not pay attention to anything other than this goal
Food is not easily digested due to utter negligence
He who lives in silence will spend a hundred years in happiness |177|

A student should give up lust, anger, and greed
He should also avoid grooming and excessive sleep
All these also disturb the concentration of the student
There is no education without punishment for local dependents |178|

Whoever eats what the earth has given itself,
Whoever dwells in the forest and lives in love,
Such a person fulfils the requirements of Pitru every day
The Vedas address such people as sages in their own way |179|

He who eats only once a day,
He who engages himself daily in eight deeds,
This person is what the Vedas call a Brahmin
He meets women only during menstruation |180|

He who does worldly duty,
He who engages in pastoral trades,
That man is what the Vedas call a vaishya
A local man must make his life fit for work |181|

For one who causes trouble in another's work,
For one who is only engaged in his own selfish pursuits,
Our Indian culture calls this person an imposter
One should be wary of those who have this character |182|

To him, who destroys the lake and the wells,
To him, who are busy demolishing temples?
Indian culture calls these people Mlecchas
One should be wary of those who are Mlecchas |183|

For one who steals the money of God and a teacher,
For one who has intercourse with another woman,
Indian culture calls these people Chandalas
Such people keep all kinds of animal's |184|

Good men donate all the wealth they earn
Along with Karna, many good men became ideal
Other people will eat the honey collected by the honey bee
The wealth that one cannot enjoy goes to someone else |185|

In a house where the waves of happiness are surging,
A home with good children and a loving wife,
A true example of wedlock in our Indian place
In such a house, the service of good men takes place |186|

Whoever is helpless should be helped
There should be an inclination towards donations
A giver will never be in the situation of asking
God gives to the donor more than what is given |187|

Gentleness among relatives, kindness among others,
Love in gentlemen, patience in teachers,
All these are the characteristics of an ideal man
It is raining on this earth because of such human's |188|

The hymns of the Vedas should be heard by ear
The eyes of good men should be seen
One should set out to visit holy places
Otherwise, one's life will be meaningless |189|

What's wrong with spring if the trees don't sprout leaves?
What is wrong with the sun if the owl is blind during the day?
What's wrong with the cloud if the rain doesn't fall on the face?
No one can change the writing on the forehead without pace |190|

Through the association of gentlemen, the wicked become good
But gentlemen will never be corrupted by the company of the wicked
The soil emancipates the fragrance of the flowers
But the flower does not emancipate the fragrance of the earth |191|

Virtue is obtained by seeing good men
Because they are the ones who save one from hardship
Holy places bear fruit after a period of time
But seeing the good men gives results in the present time |192|

A palm tree is the biggest in a village
A washer man is a big donor in a village
The greatest is the one who protects women from others
Gentlemen are not afraid even of poisonous insect's |193|

In which house Vedic mantras are not chanted,
in which house Swaha mantras are not uttered,
That house will be like a graveyard with evil bites
Because of this, the children will not get any rites |194|

Truth is the mother, and knowledge is the father
Religion is a brother, and kindness is a sister
Peace is a wife, and forgiveness is a son
These six people are the true relatives of a person |195|

Change is a constant feature of Mother Nature
Immutability is the basic nature of Dharma
Thus, life should be made of a fixed element that only appears
Everything else is seen only for a moment and then disappears |196|

A dinner invitation to Brahmins will bring happiness
A new spring pasture brings delight to the cows
A husband's enthusiasm is what makes a wife happy
It is the war that makes the valiant Kshatriya happy |197|

He who sees another woman as his mother,
He who sees the wealth of others as dust,
Essentially, they have the right vision
He sees all animals as his soul on his mission. |198|

Zealous in religion, sweet in countenance,
Enthusiastic, naive in charity, inner peace,
These are the characteristics of a good man
Such a person has devotion to Paraman |199|

If Kalpavriksha is a tree, Sumeru is a mountain
The moon will wane while the sun is bright
Thus, Sri Ramachandra cannot be compared with these
This Raghupati is a true gentleman in peace |200|

Knowledge is a friend for someone who is foreign
A wife is a real friend for her husband at home
Medicine is the friend of a sufferer
Religion is an ally as well as a life partner |201|

Don't spend money without thinking properly
One should not fight with another without a helper
Do not be hasty in any work to cherish
Those who do not do this will quickly perish |202|

The wise should not worry about their food
He should not worry about eternal nutrition
Food is already formed when the wise are born
Instead, they should think about religion |203|

The vessel fills with water dripping
Knowledge is acquired by practice
Virtue should also be collected bit by bit
Money should be earned little by little |204|

A very ripe fruit cannot become much sweeter
An evil person will not be able to attain realization in old age
Along with the body, one should correct the inner self
Instead of changing the world, one should change himself |205|

Doing good deeds and living for one moment is enough
Without wishing harm, living for one day is enough
Don't you need at least four people to take you to the cemetery?
Doing evil and living for a thousand years is not the right chemistry |206|

Thinking about the past is useless
Just thinking about the future is not right
Now think about what to do in Glad
The rest should be left to God |207|

Good men are naturally satisfied with the gods
Friends will be satisfied with good drinks
Relatives will feel satisfied with a good meal
Scholars will be enriched by the erudite deal |208|

Great ones will live as ``Parapokararthmidam Shariram''
Whenever a philanthropic question arises, they accept charity
They also use charity to do good when the poorer's ping
They are humble, even though they think money is not everything |209|

Where there is love, there is also fear
This love is always the source of suffering
Don't attach to everyone too much
Even ambrosia is poison if it is too much |210|

He who understands calamity in advance,
He who has the plan before disaster strikes,
He will find success in life by means of protection
Those who think that all this is fate will perish without inclination |211|

If the king becomes religious, the subjects will also follow religion
If the king becomes sinful, the subjects will also obey evil
Thus, the king should not be indifferent and grim
Along with the times, the country also follows him |212|

A person who lives without religion is like a dead person
A person who is religious is alive even though he is dead
If religion is protected, it will protect us forever, like a boon
Those who have been in religion will always be like the sun |213|

One should understand the religion by following it
Adhering to religion, one should understand lust
Salvation is attainable only according to religion
These are the good steps of life with perfection |214|

Those who are envious of the true glory that others have earned
taunt him when they do not receive it in this way
Selfless people do their best for people who feel sorry
Simple, innocent service brings true glory |215|

The infatuated mind is the cause of attachment
By giving up attachment, salvation can be attained
The mind can be controlled by practicing proper motivation
A clean mind leads to the attainment of salvation |216|

By practicing yoga, one's achievement matures
If the attachment to the body is gone, the mind will be right
Meditation can be done by removing physical well-being
Then this same mind will possess Samadhi with a bang |217|

We must eat what we have made in this world
So one should do well in this local mould
A calf can recognize its mother among cows
It is the karma we have done that follows us |218|

Living with dignity requires discipline and restraint
One should improve his own behavior
Life becomes difficult if you fall into ridicule
Society is a mirror of the inner self's module |219|

The earth should be dug with tools to get the water
One should dig out the knowledge of the Guru by serving him
Discipline is one of the basic qualities of the education module
Without giving up pleasure and sleep, education is not available |220|

The next move should be after considering the pros and cons
You should save money by thinking about the pros and cons
Reward is only according to one's deeds
Intelligence also depends on karmic feeds |221|

The statement ``Guru Sakshat Parabrahmah'' should be noted
Love and devotion towards the Guru should arise naturally
Even the teacher who taught a letter should be saluted
Otherwise, one will end up as a dog and will be punished |222|

Don't get distracted from the goal, no matter how many difficulties come
Don't get back from the work, no matter how many obstacles come
History says that those who behave like this are great
Strong will is the tool to overcome all obstacles' fleet |223|

Along with food, water is essential for all animals
If food is for the mind, this water is for the soul
Along with food, water is the most precious thing on earth
Fools call fragments of stone gems; they are not worth |224|

The hardships that come with poverty
Mental diseases accompanying the physical
All these are the result of one's deeds
Calamities are also from the same feeds |225|

Wealth and relatives can be regained
And this land can also be reclaimed
But it is impossible to regain human birth
It is attained after 84 lakh births |226|

A well-organized army can defeat enemy armies
A thatched roof prevents excessive rain
These are examples of the statement "strength is in unity"
A friendly atmosphere is the strength of unity in diversity |227|

The oil will double in size in the pot of water
Charity given to good people is doubled
The knowledge imparted to the Pandits doubles
Never tell your secrets to the wicked ones |228|

The feeling that arises while listening to discourses,
The feeling that arises when attending last rites,
If it remains the same, the worldly bond can be crossed
If one continues like this, he will get salvation |229|

While giving charity, displaying bravery,
While doing penance, while researching
One should never display arrogance
No one tree is bigger, which is true evidence |230|

Even being close is of no use when there is no camaraderie
He who is in the heart is far away but has no problem
True intimacy does not count on physical trends
One should develop friendships among friends |231|

Deal with those who don't like us with love and win
Make a difference with the real enemy and win
The hunter sings first and seduces the deer
Know that the enemy of the enemy is always a peer |232|

One should mix with King and Fire through the middle path
One should walk neither too far nor too close to them
Too much proximity can lead to one's destruction cult
If you move too far like that, you will not get the desired result |233|

Fire, Water, Woman, Fool, Serpent, and King's Family
One should serve all these as vigilantes
Serving is a skill on life's string
Carelessness is life-threatening |234|

If the tongue is good, the whole town will be good
It is good to speak with love among all
The truth is that no one likes abuse and pun
It is right to live in harmony with everyone |235|

One should speak according to the occasion
Dialogue should be conducted according to one's own strength
Even if the truth is to be told, it should be said pleasantly
The right person is the one who expresses his anger properly |236|

Even though the object is the same, the vision is different
A female body feels like a corpse to a yogi
The same body feels like lust for a man
As there is vision, there is creation |237|

Do not claim the medicine you have made for yourself
Even family secrets should not be attributed to anyone
Don't reveal your secrets when you are in crisis
If you want to live decently, you should behave like this |238|

The cuckoo sings only in the spring
At all other times, one hears the cawing of crows
One should wait for the right time to do all the work
Sometimes silence, meditation, and speech are needed |239|

Money and wealth can be obtained from Dharma
Dharma is accumulated by money and wealth
These are interdependent in life's strife
This is the real meaning of life |240|

Keeps company with the good while forsaking the evil
Dispel the illusion of family and meditate on God
Peace can be found only by leaving the company of evildoers
Life can be sanctified by thinking of divine invaders |241|

To him who wishes good for all things,
For one who sees the Lord in all beings in the world,
There is no need to wear any religion cosmetics
It is the hallmark of a great man in local politics |242|

The company of the wicked is an invitation to disaster
It is a misadventure that provokes unwanted troubles
Everyone should be saved from evil trouble
Keep as much distance from them as possible |243|

Cleanliness of the body is dear to God
The inner mind is happy with all the cleanliness
Eat to live, but please don't live to eat
Do not sleep after sunrise for achievement |244|

If you have money, you will have many relatives
Where money is paramount, everything else is secondary
If there is no money, everyone makes you sit on your knee
If there is money, they will surround you like a honey bee |245|

Work and live on the path of truth and Dharma
We must do our duty without leaving
Ill-earned money lasts only a short time
Later, the money will not help for prime time |246|

Even the evil deed of one who is capable feels good
But the good deed of someone who is incompetent looks bad
Even ambrosia has become poison for Rahu
The quality of the act will be decided by the occasion |247|

A meal is what remains after being eaten by the guest
Friendship is love and trust expressed in another
He who never commits sin has good charectory
The true Dharma is a life without adultery |248|

Even if a gem is kicked in the foot, its value will not decrease
If the glass is carried on the head, its price does not increase
Always genuine is genuine; fake is fake
A crow is a crow, and a cuckoo is a cuckoo |249|

Indian Vedic scriptures are very numerous
Here, education disciplines are also very numerous
Thus, the student should absorb only the essence
Swans only suck milk in watery milk |250|

The one who comes unexpectedly tired should be treated first
He should be fed first to the satisfaction of one's inner nest
The rest should be eaten later by the master of the house
One should understand the statement "Atithi Devo Bhava" |251|

Those who have studied the four Vedas
must first realize God as the soul form in the heart
If not, all knowledge will be wasted in his lifetime
It is like losing taste buds during good mealtime |252|

Brahmins are ascetics and study the Vedas
They are always capable of leading society
Their mission is the welfare of the world
Those who insult them will perish, as Veda told |253|

The moon in the sky will be very bright
But he loses his brilliance in front of the sun
A dog becomes a lion only in its own street
It stamps its tail on another's street |254|

The happiness found in one's own home is different
The comfort found in someone else's place is different
Adapting to the situation is smart
A bee also sits on a curry flower in drought |255|

There are many types of bonds in this world
Love and romantic bonds are very powerful
Bees bore even the big trees within an hour
But it becomes inactive in the lotus flower |256|

Even if a sandalwood tree is cut, it does not lose its fragrance
Even when the elephant Is old, it does not give up its gestures
Good men never leave their nobility, even in poverty
They will endure everything by thinking it is God's charity |257|

In life, there are meanings like Dharma, Artha, Kama, and Moksha
There is a heaven's gate to enter for one who lives in righteousness
This is how one's welfare takes place in this factorial
Sages have said this since time immemorial |258|

He who is engrossed in the pleasures will face hundreds of calamities
Who will remain close to the king of this world till the end?
A beggar will never get respect from anyone or fame
Thus, one should spend his life in remembrance of God's name |259|

The existence of the golden deer is not in this creation
In this world, no one has ever seen it
Even so, Rama chased after it with a theme
In bad times, the intellect becomes extreme |260|

A person looks good because of his virtues
One recognizes him even though he is in a low position
Be serious, no matter whether you are in any position
You shouldn't be proud after getting a good position. |261|

A diamond does not perceive itself as precious
Kasturi does not appreciate itself as Wahl!
It is polite not to paint oneself
It is only when others describe you that it has value |262|

All the virtues are also with the wise
All vices are with a fool
Virtue and wisdom are two sides of the same coin
Diamonds are adorned with gold when they join |263|

Difficulties always come to fellow gentlemen
This complex question is a head-scratcher
A legacy of these hardships will come for purity
Ishan never tests the wicked; see this for clarity |264|

When wealth comes, charity should be done
It should be understood that everyone has an equal share
"Bahujana Hitaya Bahujana Sukhaya" should be understood
No matter how much milk a dog has at its breast |265|

There is no limit to human desires
No matter what, there is no satisfaction
These happiness and satisfactions are in our vector
Life becomes worthwhile when what comes to Paul is nectar |266|

Charity should be given only to those who are in need
Shelter should be given to those who have surrendered
This is the fundamental ethos of Indian culture
If this happens, everyone will benefit in the future |267|

Grass is the lightest in this world
Cotton is lighter than this in this world
A beggar is lighter than both of them
One's own existence is ruined by begging |268|

Everyone likes someone who is happy all the time
Everyone wants to be connected with him
One should behave courteously with one another
Like this, the public can gain success in the future |269|

This non-violence is the true religion of man
Love and trust are the secrets of success
It is said that if played, it should be like a pearl necklace
One should not hurt anyone in words, body, or mind's space |270|

A man should practice good rituals
Study, japa, penance, and charity should be done
Good rituals help a person in his rebirth
Such a mind finds peace and tranquilly in depth |271|

What is the use of not reading the teachings in the scriptures?
What good is it if one loses money when he is in trouble?
 Knowledge must be mastered for benefits
One should save money for his debts |272|

Whoever does not learn through a teacher,
Who understands knowledge by reading a book
Such people do not thrive under scholars' hats
They do not get respect like harlot shots |273|

Benevolence should be shown to those who have done good
Violence should be done to those who have done violence
In doing so, it is not sternness
It is right to resist evil with firmness |274|

In attaining that which is far away?
In earning worship by doing the impossible,
All these can be obtained through penance
Nothing equals the power of penance |275|

There is no need for other vices before greed
There is no need for sin before the nature of insulting others
If you have a pure mind, there is no need for holy baths
There is no need for politeness on good paths |276|

He who is weak will always be a sentient
Whoever has no money will remain unmarried
A patient becomes a devotee of God
When a woman grows old, she remains loyal to her husband |277|

There is no other charity equal to the donation of food
There is no other date equal to Dwadashi
There is no other mantra equal to Gayatri
There is no other god equal to Savitri |278|

The poison of a serpent is in its teeth
The poison of the fly is in its scalp
But the poison of the wicked is in his whole body
So, they feel happy when they hurt somebody |279|

The hand is beautified by charity
Bathing cleanses the body
Peace of mind is obtained from honors
Man can live happily through good manners |280|

The scarlet gourd destroys the intellect
Affectionate speech enhances the intellect
Thus, everything should be pleasant and moderate
Only then will life be happy and delightful |281|

This body should be reserved for philanthropy
The prosperity of others should be seen as one's own prosperity
Eternal nutrition is also done by animals and birds
But a man must overcome this without words |282|

A sense of philanthropy is conscious in the heart of a gentleman
Thus, they remain far away without being affected by losses
Man should live as harmoniously as possible
Otherwise, living on this planet becomes impossible |283|

When there is a soft-spoken wife at home,
When a humble son is accompanied by a grandson,
Such a happy creature is not present even in Indra's world
This is the formula for a happy family in the local mould |284|

Food, sleep, fear, and mating are present in all animals
In addition to this, human beings have a passion for knowledge
A man without knowledge is just like an animal
"Nahi Gnyene Sadrisham" has to be seen in formal |285|

Death

Oh dear, DEATH is not the end
Rather, it is just a hairpin bend
Why do you fear this auspicious fact?
Welcome to this act gracefully with tact |1|

Oh dear DEATH is a real celebration
Just nothing but a true convocation
It is just an ending of measurable known
And is the introduction to immeasurable unknown |2|

Oh dear DEATH is a just a natural process
So please look at the transition as success
Transformation and tessellation are inevitable to everyone
Why do you worry it is just an end of local geometrical projection |3|

Oh dear DEATH is an immense opportunity for your evolution
It is a true holy event which cares for your internal summation
So the rituals and reformation are in many forms in the process of it
At the edge of life you definitely going to understand it |4|

Oh dear DEATH and birth are nothing but an integer
It continues even after the ending of local procedure
So consider enlightenment and emancipation when you're living
And show respect and compassion towards all beings |5|

Oh dear, the edges of DEATH is prevalent for your inner mind
With sensory perception you are enveloped with the illusionary bind
The one who is aware can prepare the self for this unavoidable event
And look inward if he keeps his mind only in the present |6|

Oh dear, why are you waiting for DEATH to happen
Every moment you are dying if you are living in fear
You are a structure of physical, mental, and divine origin
So death is an address to achieve a different structure again |7|

Oh dear, please invite DEATH like a life with an open arm
Please understand the reality then there will be no harm
Remember you are a knight so don't be afraid of flight
If you are confused, then you will have to face a big fight |8|

Oh dear, in DEATH only the local mind will disappear
But the total inner being will unfold for you in its original flavour
What you are conscious now is just a fragment of the whole
What you going to get will be an amazing pure void bowl |9|

Oh dear, DEATH is the door to enter the pure consciousness
The Pranava AUM is the key to go beyond this local awareness
Situational and conditional are just an intellectual local creativeness
Going beyond time and space is possible only by fundamental activeness |10|

Oh dear, DEATH is narrated in many age-old scriptures
But they never describe it in the domain of pure awareness
You need to observe the observer inside, just as a witness
Never follow anything or anyone other than self-religiousness|11|

Oh dear, DEATH cannot be learned from any kind of mediation
But it can only be realized only through unifying meditation
Know that meditation is neither concentration nor a progression
It is just a happening beyond any kind of logical interpretation |12|

Oh dear, DEATH is not just knowledge because it is not an analysis
It is a flower that blossoms, and a certain kind of synthesis
Death is a movement from dual to non-dual through integrality
It is so marvellous by the grace of ultimatum in the form of singularity |13|

Oh dear, DEATH is the caution under the law of causality
It is just an occasion to complete the local formality
But nobody is here or elsewhere to guide you in this local cessation
You have to die when you live here, for your future allocation |14|

Oh dear, DEATH is not surely the end of your inner witness
But you should die hard to understand this with the happiness
So wake up and make up your mind by showing your true guts
Face death bravely by cracking these social ruts |15|

Oh dear, be happy because DEATH shows you your true form
To understand that, you have to practice a new norm
If you really die consciously with full awareness
Ultimate will surely give you a choice to blossom in blissfulness |16|

Oh dear, once again I'm telling you DEATH is inevitable
So get the awareness and consciousnesses as quickly as possible
Achieving awareness in wakefulness, dream and deep sleep
Live life fully and embrace DEATH with Grace |17|

<h1 align="center"><u>So Far</u></h1>

Awards: Best Paper Award - 2017
Young Scientist Award - 2019
Adhyatmika Ratna Awarad – 2021
Abraham Lincoln Excellence Awarad - 2023

Research Paper Publication [ISSN: 2249-5754]: 14 Nos.
Publications in English / Kannada: 28 Nos.
[notionpress.com/Amazonian/flipchart]

<h2 align="center">Utkarshanam</h2>

Psycho-somatic wellness centre

Ph: 74114 04535
E-mail: kaushalamngo@gmail.com
You tube: **Dr.Chandra Mouli M S**